DAILY SENSORIMOTOR TRAINING ACTIVITIES

A Handbook

for

Teachers and Parents

of

Pre-School Children

William T. Braley, M.Ed.
Geraldine Konicki
Catherine Leedy

EDUCATIONAL ACTIVITIES, INC., FREEPORT, L.I., NEW YORK

Illustrations by Cathy Galterio

Printed in the
United States of America

Library of Congress Catalog Number 1017-56181
ISBN 0-914296-03-5

SENSORIMOTOR ACTIVITIES FOR TEACHERS AND PARENTS OF PRE-SCHOOL CHILDREN

PREFACE

The purpose of this manual is to present sensorimotor activities for the pre-school child. The activities are designed to be integrated with the curriculum and equipment used in pre-school centers. Parents will find that many of the activities can be done easily in the home.

The material is presented in such a way that the classroom teacher can follow a daily lesson plan of activities. Comprehensive evaluations are included at the end of each week so that the teacher may check her class' progress during the thirty-four week training period.

The authors would like to thank two individuals, Mrs. Ann Graham and Mrs. Nancy Mukes, for their help in the collection and selection of the activities in the text.

We would also like to thank Miss Barbara Schnelle, Coordinator of the Early Childhood Education Project, Dayton Public Schools, for permitting the authors to institute this program successfully with some 1800 three-, four- and five-year-old children enrolled in this program. She also aided the authors in innumerable other ways, in order that the sensorimotor phase of the project could be carried out.

INTRODUCTION

The need for pre-school children to be provided with a varied sensorimotor environment can best be met by having the children participate in daily classroom experiences aimed at developing sensory acuity and motor skills.

An increasing awareness of the need for stimulation of the senses in young children is becoming more and more evident among the members of various disciplines throughout the country. This stimulation must take place during the formative period, from birth to age six.

Educators, Child Development Specialists, Psychologists, Neurologists, Pediatricians and others are seeking through research to discover how sensorimotor training can help children to achieve more significantly in academic situations. Although there are many conflicting theories and claims, many of which are not backed by scientific research, we feel that there is enough evidence to support a program of the type outlined in this manual.

The rationale for this program is based upon observations made by Heron, Piaget, Montessori, Getman, Gesell, and others. A broad encompassing statement about their findings would serve to point out that the acquisition of sensorimotor skills is essential to the young child's understanding of and adjustment to the world of persons, things, and ideas.

It is known that there are many children who have been denied the experiences necessary for proper development of sensorimotor experiences. These children may fall under one or more of the following categories:

1. Children having some type of cerebral or neurological dysfunction.
2. Culturally disadvantaged children who have been denied natural childhood experiences.
3. Children who have suffered a severe emotional upset.
4. Children who have had their natural instinct toward pursuing their own developmental processes stifled by over-protective parents.

We feel that a preventive type of program designed to help pre-school children overcome deficits that might have developed in the sensorimotor areas, will help them to become more perceptually aware. This awareness will enable them to cope more easily with the academic programs of the first grade. It is almost impossible to go back and try to help a child "make up" for experiences that he may have missed.

A promising feature of this program is involved with its effect upon the child's feeling about himself. The child, who undertakes the activities outlined in the manual, is able to perform in areas which help to build his self image. The curriculum is designed to appeal to the child's natural instinct for play, giving the child an opportunity to succeed in a familiar environment. Once a child succeeds in any task it helps him to become more emotionally stable. Stressful situations occur as a child reaches the first grade and is asked to learn to read and write. The development of good self-image can help a child to overcome this stress.

Dr. Gertrude Justison in "The Montessori Handbook" states:

> "If, indeed, learning is predicated on movement...if interaction with the environment is essential for gathering information and storing it in experiential unit for future reference...if out of movement patterns comes a system of "perceptual match" relationships pre-requisite to concepts formation...if spatial, form, and time concepts are nurtured in the direct bodily movements through space and time in patterned directions in early life experiences; then reevaluation of pedagogical practices is long overdue, and the translation of known psychophysiological principles in action programs is crucial in an increasingly complex world."

Although many of the skills developed in this program are not new to education, we feel that many teachers should be encouraged to reevaluate the need for "educating the body" before attempting to ask the child to achieve in academic work.

William Braley
Geraldine Konicki
Catherine Leedy

INDEX

BODY IMAGE

Children need to discover how their bodies move, they have to be able to "sort out" one part of their body from another and they should be able to distinguish between right and left when they enter the first grade.

We know that children start to develop an awareness of their bodies during infancy. In order that this awareness can be developed to the highest degree, the training procedures described in this section may be used.

If a child develops a good image of his body, he will have a sound base upon which to build the perceptual skills which will be needed in future classroom activities.

Supply the children with large sheets of paper and crayons. Ask the children to draw a picture of themselves. It is suggested that the teacher keep this paper for future evaluation.

Identify Body Parts - The teacher touches the different parts of the body and says, "This is my head; touch your head." Continue, using the following:

- mouth
- ears
- chin
- neck
- shoulders
- arms
- elbows
- legs
- ankles
- toes
- wrists
- hands
- fingers
- chest
- stomach
- back
- hips
- knees
- feet
- heels

Teacher instructs children to touch body parts on command. For example: "Place both hands on your head." Continue using the following:

mouth	wrists
ears	hands
chin	fingers
neck	chest
shoulders	stomach
arms	back
elbows	hips
legs	knees
ankles	feet
toes	heels

Teacher asks the children to close their eyes and instructs them to touch the parts of their body on command. Use all of the following:

- mouth
- ears
- chin
- neck
- shoulders
- arms
- elbows
- legs
- ankles
- toes
- wrists
- hands
- fingers
- chest
- stomach
- back
- hips
- knees
- feet
- heels

Children touch body parts with other body parts:

nose to knee
chin to chest
ear to shoulder
hands to hips
elbows to knees
toes to nose
wrist to ear
elbow to leg
chin to wrist
wrist to ankle
fingers to shoulders
wrist to back
elbow to stomach
wrist to neck
foot to leg
hands to back
toes to toes
heels to heel

WEEK 2
MONDAY

This day is to be used for evaluation of what the children have learned during the past week. It is important that the children have a clear understanding of the body parts and their location.

The evaluation should take the form of an individual objective check list for each child. This check list will give an indication of how well the children have mastered knowledge of body parts. This check list can serve as a guide to the teacher for all future training and review. Do NOT expect each child to become proficient in knowing all of the body parts.

An example of a check list for the first week follows. Instruct children to sit down and close their eyes. Touch these parts of the body on command:

mouth
feet
back
hands
eyes
stomach
ears

Review other activities from the previous week.

Touch Body Parts to Surroundings: Teacher asks child to touch:

head to floor
hands to wall
elbows to chalkboard
knees to floor
head to table or desk
back to wall
ankles to wall

nose to window
ear to chair
shoulder to floor
fingers to books
chest to desks
wrist to chalkboard
stomach to floor

Children imitate teacher in the movement of a specific body part. Always identify the part. Examples:

Nod your head
Close your eyes
Twist your neck
Bend your elbows
Clap your hands
Wiggle your toes

Wiggle your nose
Open your mouth
Shrug your shoulders
Click your fingers
Bend your knees
Stamp your feet

Teacher instructs the children to move specific body parts on command.
Do NOT demonstrate.

Nod your head
Close your eyes
Twist your neck
Bend your elbows
Clap your hands
Wiggle your toes

Wiggle your nose
Open your mouth
Shrug your shoulders
Click your fingers
Bend your knees
Stamp your feet

State the usage of the body part and let the children supply the name.

I see with my ______________
I smell with my ______________
I blink my ______________
I talk with my ______________
I clap with my ______________
I snap my ______________
I walk with my ______________
I wave my ______________
I shrug my ______________
I jump with my ______________
I write with my ______________

Have children perform these tasks.

This day is to be used for evaluation of what the children have learned during the past week. It is important that the children have a clear understanding of the body parts and their location.

The evaluation should take the form of an individual objective check list for each child. This check list will give an indication of how well the children have mastered the knowledge of body parts. The check list can serve as a guide to the teacher for all future training and review. Do NOT expect each child to become proficient in knowing all of the body parts.

An example of a check list for the second week follows. Instruct children to sit down and close their eyes. Touch these parts of the body:

- shoulders
- legs
- arms
- toes
- chest
- knees
- fingers

Review other activities from the previous week.

Teacher places a piece of paper as large as a child on the floor. One child lies on his back on the paper while another child draws around him, making the outline of his body. Each child should have the experience of drawing around another child and seeing himself on paper.

Instruct the children to color a designated part of the outlined body a specific color.

EXAMPLE: Color the feet yellow, the toes blue, the legs orange, the ankles green, the knees red, etc.

Collect pictures of specific body parts and ask the children to identify them.

Paste a picture of a specific body part (such as a nose) on a sheet of paper. Instruct the children to draw a complete person around this part.

Draw an incomplete man on the chalkboard or on paper and ask the children to supply the missing parts.

To emphasize body parts, teach the children to do the "Hokey Pokey." See Educational Activities record EALP #601.

Cut up paper dolls and put them into envelopes. Distribute the envelopes to the children and ask them to re-assemble the paper doll.

To emphasize body parts, teach the children to do the "Looby Lou."

SPACE AND DIRECTION

After developing the awareness of body image a child must be able to identify his body position with that of his surroundings (space). He must also realize the course of movement which he must follow in order to change from his present position to his destination (direction).

The child's awareness of space and direction helps him to read from left to right and to place written thoughts on paper in an organized manner.

Encourage creative movement. Use your whole room. Use your own imagination! Do not demonstrate! Examples:

Show me how small you can be (also, how tall, wide, tall and thin, long and thin).

Point to the farthest wall; touch it and return to your own place.

Point to the nearest wall; touch it and return to your own place.

Standing in your own place, make your feet move fast; slow.

Move your hands fast; slow.

Show me how slow you can walk.

Show me how fast you can walk.

Be a tree, wall, ball, river.

Direct the children to point: in front of them, in back of them, to the side of them, to the top and bottom of objects in the room.

Children, with eyes closed, point to objects in the room. Examples: point to the door, chalkboard, flag, window, wastebasket, floor, ceiling, cupboards, etc.

Direct the children to point above, below, over, under and between objects in the room.
Examples:

over the door	over your shoulder
below the window	above the pictures
under the chair	below the chalkboard
between the desks	over the wastebasket
under the desk	between the books

Direct the children to move designated body parts in a specific direction.
Examples:

Put your finger up
Put your head down
Put your arms between your legs
Put your fingers under your feet
Put your elbows below your hips
Put your feet over your head
Put your arms in back of you
Put your hands in front of you
Put your arms in back of your legs
Put both hands on the same side of you
Point both hands to one side of you

Direct the children to move their bodies in relation to objects in the room.
Examples:

Stand in front of your table
Stand with the windows in back of you
Stand so that the flag is to your side
Move so that you are under a table
Move so that you are under a chair
Move so that the door is in front of you
Move so that the door is behind you
Move so that you are between two chairs

Set up an obstacle course. Include something to crawl through (cardboard boxes), to walk under (a pole or stick), to squeeze through (two desks or chairs), to step over (a pole or stick), to step into (a rope or tape circle).

Use verbal commands, making sure that the children understand the different directions to follow while taking the prescribed route through the obstacle course.

WEEK 5
MONDAY

Instruct children to close their eyes and point to familiar objects throughout the room. Examples: clock, door, flag, chalkboard, piano, windows, teacher's desk, floor, library table, etc. This activity is used to check and develop their awareness of their environment and the directions of their movements in relation to their surroundings.

Instruct children to jump, and while in air, turn toward objects in the room. Turn toward the door, window, chalkboard, clock, flag, piano, teacher's desk, etc.

Instruct children to close their eyes. Children jump, and while in air, turn toward objects in the room. Turn toward the door, window, chalkboard, clock, flag, piano, teacher's desk, bulletin board, etc.

Instruct children to jump and, while in air, turn toward different sides of the room. Examples: door side, window side, clock side, bulletin board side, chalkboard side, flag side, piano side, etc.

Instruct children to close their eyes and raise the right or left hands.

Instruct children to raise right or left legs. The eyes are closed during this activity, also. This will test the children's directional awareness and their sense of balance.

Teachers should always use the terms "right" and "left" when asking the children to line up for leaving the room or for playing games.

Instruct children to follow such directions as:

1. Walk sideways
2. Walk backward
3. Walk forward
4. Hop to the right
5. Hop to the left
6. Hop forward
7. Hop backward
8. Skip forward
9. Skip backward
10. Jump sideways
11. Run forward
12. Run backward
13. Run to the right
14. Run to the left
15. March forward
16. March backward
17. Tiptoe to the right
18. Tiptoe to the left
19. Tiptoe forward
20. Tiptoe backward

Instruct children to point to different sides of their bodies. Examples:

1. Look to the left side of body
2. Look to the right side of body
3. Point to the right side of your head
4. Point to the left side of your head
5. Point to your right foot
6. Point to your left foot
7. Touch your right shoulder

Instruct children to point to the right and turn in a complete circle to the right.

Instruct children to point to the left and turn in a complete circle to the left.

Instruct children to walk:

1. To the right
2. To the left
3. Forward
4. Backward

Ask children to creep:

1. To the right
2. To the left
3. Forward
4. Backward

WEEK 5
FRIDAY

This day is to be used for evaluation of what the child has learned during the past weeks.

Use this check list for evaluation.

Ask the children to close their eyes and point:

Up	To their hips	To their chin
Down	To their ankles	To their neck
In front of them	To their wrists	
Behind them	To their heels	

Ask the children to:

Stand in front of their chairs
Stand so that the door is behind them
Walk sideways
Tiptoe backward

BALANCE

Balance is the ability of the child to sustain control of his body when using both sides simultaneously, individually, or alternately.

The ability to balance is essential to all basic locomotor tasks.

If a child has good balance, his body can act in an integrated manner, freeing his mind to concentrate on abstract matters.

Children assume hand and knee positions on the floor.

1. Each child raises one hand in the air. Alternate hands.
2. Each child raises one leg in the air. Alternate legs.
3. Each child raises right arm and right leg. Alternate legs.
4. Children raise alternate hands and legs in the air, right arms and left legs.
5. Children raise left arms and right legs, slowly.

<u>Walking Board Activity</u> (See Appendix)
Children walk forward on walking board. Children walk slowly, one foot in front of the other, heel to toe. Arms are held at a natural position at sides. Eyes are focused on the end of the walking board.

WEEK 6
TUESDAY

1. Children balance on tiptoes for the count of ten.
2. Children each stand on one foot for the count of five. Alternate feet.
3. Children rise from a sitting position on the floor, keeping arms folded on the chest.

Walking Board Activities

1. Children walk backward on the walking board, slowly.
2. Children walk sideways on the walking board. First, right side of body leads and then left.

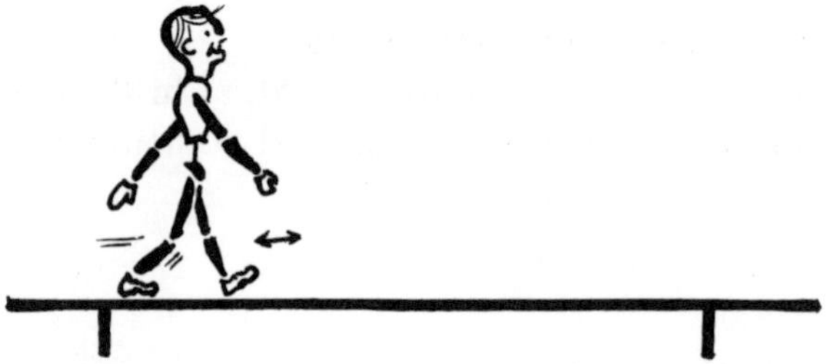

1. Rocking horse - Children stand with hands on hips and feet astride. Children lean forward, keeping knees stiff. Lift heels from the floor. Rock backward, lifting toes from the floor.

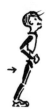

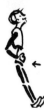

2. Elephant walk - Children bend forward from the waist, allowing arms to hang limply with hands clasped. Walk forward by taking big steps.

Walking Board Activity

Children walk to the middle of the board, moving in a forward motion. When children reach the middle, they turn one half way around and continue to the end of the board, moving in a backward motion.

WEEK 6
THURSDAY

1. Children walk forward on their knees.
2. Children walk backward on their knees.

Walking Board Activities

1. Children walk forward, keeping one foot always in front. Alternate feet.
2. Children walk backward, keeping the same foot always in back. Alternate feet.
3. Children walk forward with hands clasped behind their bodies.
4. Children walk backward with hands clasped behind their bodies.
5. Children walk forward with arms folded on chest.
6. Children walk backward with arms folded on chest.

WEEK 6
FRIDAY

This day is to be used for evaluation of what the children have learned during the past weeks.

Ask the children to stand on tiptoes, with eyes closed, for 10 seconds.
Ask the children to stand on one foot, eyes open, for 10 seconds.
Ask the children to stand on one foot, eyes closed, for 10 seconds.

Ask the children to point:

Over the door
Below the window
Under the desk
Between the desks

Ask the children to:

Put their elbows on the floor
Stand between two chairs
Jump and turn in the air toward something on the right side of the room
Place their wrist on the floor
Place their head on their knee

1. Crab walk - Children sit on the floor, placing hands on floor behind them. Raise body so that they are standing on hands and feet. Walk on hands and feet in a backward direction. Move slowly.

2. Frog Squat - Children assume a squatting position, placing hands on hips. One leg is extended to the side and then returned. Repeat with other leg, with a hopping motion.

3. Bunny hop - Children place hands at the sides of their heads, forming rabbit ears. Hop forward, keeping both feet together.

WEEK 7
TUESDAY

1. Children stand on the right foot. They hold their arms at their sides. All eyes are closed. The teacher counts to five.
2. Children stand on their left foot. Their arms are at their sides and their eyes are closed. The teacher counts to five.
3. Children stand on their tiptoes, with their eyes closed. The teacher counts to five.

Walking Board Activities

1. Children walk forward with their arms straight over their head.
2. Children walk backward with their arms straight over their head.

1. Children stand on their right foot. Their arms are folded and their eyes are closed. The teacher counts to five.
2. Children stand on their left foot. Their arms are folded and their eyes are closed. The teacher counts to five.
3. Children fold their arms and close their eyes. In this position, they jump on both feet.

Walking Board Activities

1. Children walk forward with an eraser balanced on top of their head.
2. Children walk backward with an eraser balanced on top of their head.

1. Children jump on their right foot with eyes closed.
2. Children jump on their left foot with their eyes closed.
3. Children stand on both feet with eyes closed. Instruct them to jump and turn, while in air. Use 1/4 and 1/2 turns only.

1/4 turn

1/2 turn

<u>Walking Board Activities</u>

1. Children walk forward with arms held straight out in front.
2. Children walk backward with arms held straight out in front.
3. Children walk forward with arms held straight out in front. Balance an eraser on the tops of their hands.
4. Children walk backward with arms held straight out in front. Balance an eraser on the tops of their hands.

1. Children stand on their right foot with eyes closed. Instruct them to jump and turn, while in air. Use 1/4 and 1/2 turns only.
2. Children stand on left foot with eyes closed. Instruct them to jump and turn, while in air. Use 1/4 and 1/2 turns only.

1/4 turn

1/2 turn

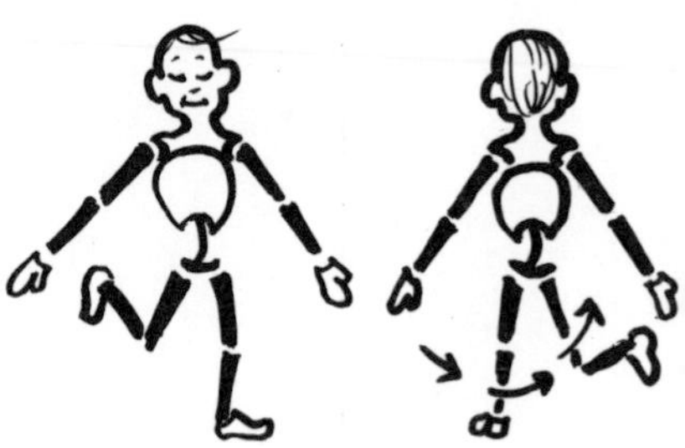

Walking Board Activities

1. Children walk forward with arms held out straight from shoulders. Balance an eraser on the palm of each hand.
2. Children walk backwards with arms held out straight from shoulders. Balance an eraser on the palm of each hand.

Balance Board (See Appendix)

1. Children stand on the boards and maintain balance.
2. Children stand on the boards and tip them to the right. Balance again.
3. Children stand on the boards and tip them to the left. Balance again.
4. Children stand on the boards and touch different parts of their body on command. Balance all of the time. Touch:

knees	shoulders
toes	elbows
head	ankles
heels	hips
wrists	

Ladder Activities - any flat ladder will do. The ladder should be placed flat on the floor.

1. Children walk forward with one foot on each side of the ladder.
2. Children walk forward on the right side of the ladder.
3. Children walk forward on the left side of the ladder.
4. Children walk forward stepping in the spaces between the rungs. This checks the child's awareness of space and direction as well as balance.
5. Children walk backward stepping in the spaces between the rungs.

Ladder Activities - The ladder is placed flat on the floor.

1. Children walk forward by stepping on each rung.
2. Children walk backward by stepping on each rung. This activity is excellent for emphasizing space awareness also.
3. Place the ladder against the wall at varying degrees of steepness. Children climb up and down. Teacher stands at the bottom of the ladder in order to brace it.

Twist Board (See Appendix)

Children stand on the boards. With arms outstretched, twist back and forth. Children will twist from the waist. This twisting motion can be obtained by placing the right hand on the left side of the body and by pushing the hand back to the right side. Repeat with left hand.

Children twist continually to the right (turning in a complete circle). This is achieved by pushing with only the left hand.

Children twist continually to the left (turning in a complete circle). This is achieved by pushing with only the right hand, across the body.

Children squat on twist boards and attempt to twist back and forth and in complete circles.

WEEK 8
FRIDAY

This day is to be used for an accumulative evaluation of all balance activities.

1. Children stand on tiptoes with eyes closed. Teacher counts for five seconds.
2. Children alternate standing on right and left foot with eyes closed for five seconds.
3. Children rise from a sitting position on the floor, keeping arms folded on chest.
4. Children stand on both feet, with eyes closed. Instruct them to jump and turn, while in air. Use 1/4 and 1/2 turns only.

<u>Walking Board</u>

1. Children walk forward with arms held out straight from shoulders. Balance an eraser on palm of each hand.
2. Children walk forward with an eraser on top of their head.

BASIC BODY MOVEMENT

When a child can move skillfully and freely, his mind will be free to interpret information transmitted to him from his surroundings.

Training in basic body movement provides the child with the ability to play games and activities, which help him achieve status among his classmates.

Through movement the child further learns about his body and its relationship to space and direction.

WEEK 9
MONDAY

Children lie on their backs on the floor, arms at sides, and feet together.

1. Children lift their heads and look at their toes. Return heads to the floor. Repeat several times.

2. Children roll their heads to the left, placing their ears on the floor. Roll heads to the right, placing ears on floor.

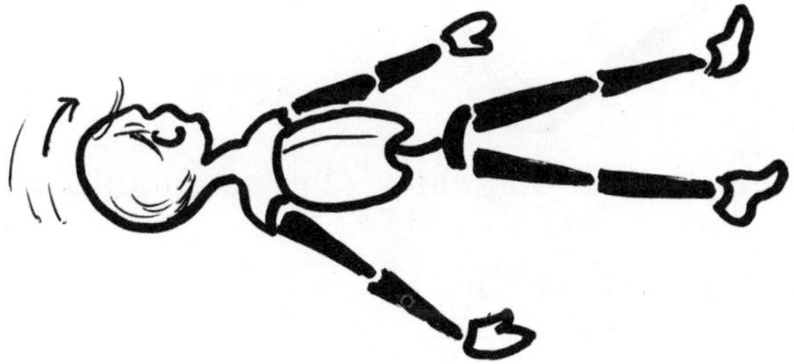

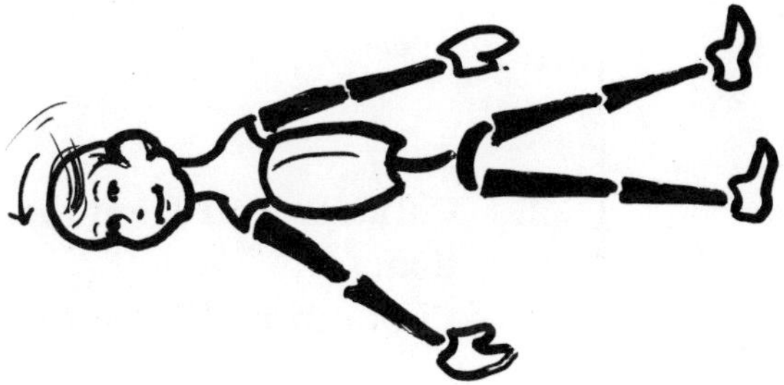

Children lie on their backs on the floor, arms at sides, and feet together.

1. Children roll their heads to the right and back to center, picking heads up to look at their toes. Replace heads to floor and roll them all the way to the left. Reverse.

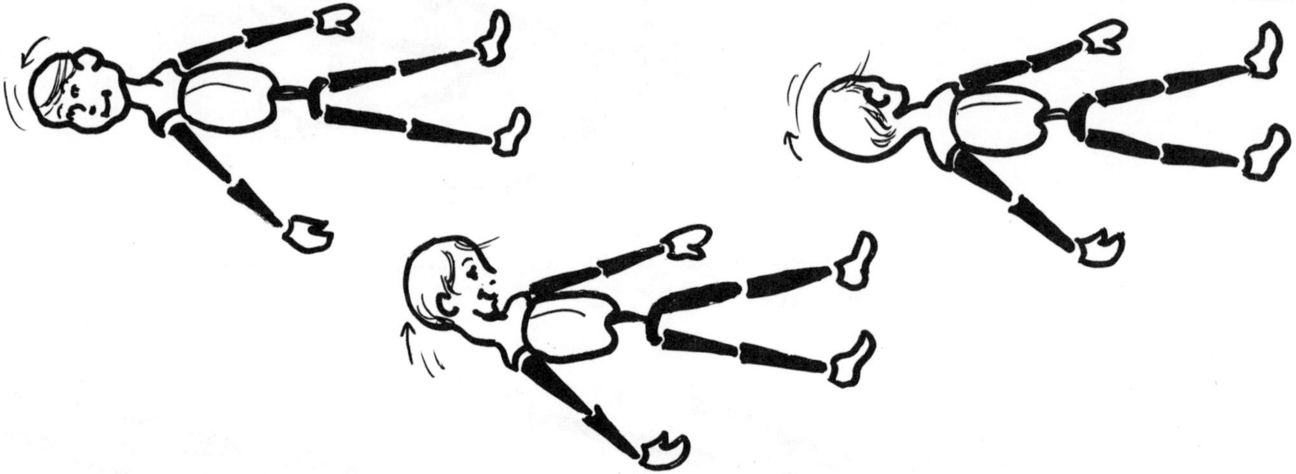

2. Children roll from their backs to their stomachs. (Try to establish right and left direction.)
3. Children roll from their stomachs to their backs.

1. Snake - Children lie on their backs, arms together overhead. Bend at hips and waists, moving body to right and left.
2. Fish - Children lie on their stomachs and imitate a fish swimming.

Snake

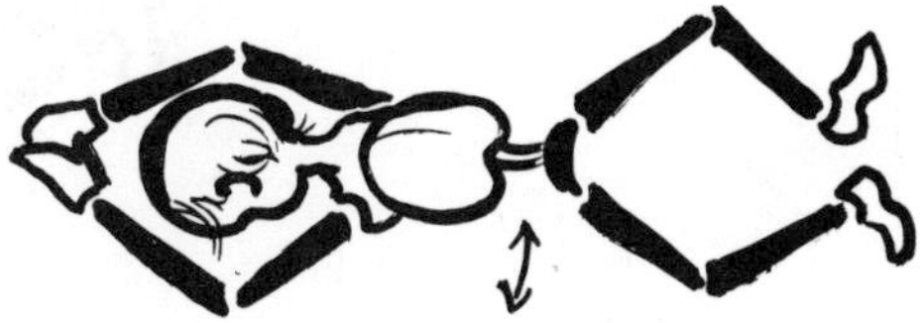

Fish

3. Bear Walk - Children assume hands and knees position. Move right legs and right arms, left arms and left legs. Walk slowly, imitating a bear.

Bear Walk

1. Children assume hands and knees position. Children slowly move right arms and left legs, left arms and right legs. Move forward.

2. Children assume hands and knees position. Children slowly move right arms and left legs, left arms and right legs in a backward direction.

3. Children, still in hands and knees position, move arms and legs sideways. Move sidewise.

WEEK 9
FRIDAY

This day is to be used for an evaluation of what the children have learned during the past week.

1. Children roll their heads to the right and back to center, picking heads up to look at their toes. Place heads back on floor and roll all the way to the left. Reverse.
2. Children roll from their backs to their stomachs. Ask them to roll to the right and then to the left.
3. Children assume hands and knees position. Move right arms and left legs, left arms and right legs. Move forward and backwards.

WEEK 10
MONDAY

1. Children practice walking. Make sure that arms and legs alternate and swing freely. Music may be used to encourage the children to move more freely.
   a. Children walk fast
   b. Children walk slowly
2. Children walk on tiptoes with arms over head.
3. Children walk backward bringing knees up high.

WEEK 10
TUESDAY

1. Children walk sideways using shuffle (slide) steps.

2. Children walk sideways using crossover steps.

3. Children walk backward on tiptoes with arms overhead.

4. Children walk in a squatting position.

5. Children alternate between walking "small" (squatting) and walking "tall" (tiptoes).

1. Children place big toes together and walk.

2. Children place heels together and walk.

3. Children walk on heels. Walk slow and fast.

4. Children walk, imitating "slow motion."

1. Children walk sideways with arms folded on chest. Use shuffle steps.

2. Children walk sideways with arms folded on chest. Use crossover steps.

3. Children walk sideways with arms behind their back. Use shuffle steps.

4. Children walk sideways with arms behind their back. Use crossover steps.

WEEK 10
FRIDAY

This day is to be used for an evaluation of what the children have learned during the last week

1. Children walk on tiptoes, hands overhead (slowly).
2. Children walk sideways, using crossover steps.
3. Children walk backwards on tiptoes with arms overhead (slowly).
4. Children place big toes together and walk.
5. Children place heels together and walk.
6. Children walk sideways with arms behind their back--use slide step.
7. Children walk sideways with arms behind their back--use crossover steps.

WEEK 11
MONDAY

1. Children practice running fast.

2. Children practice running slowly.

3. Children run with hands on their hips.

4. Children run with hands over their heads.

WEEK 11
TUESDAY

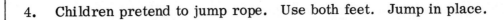

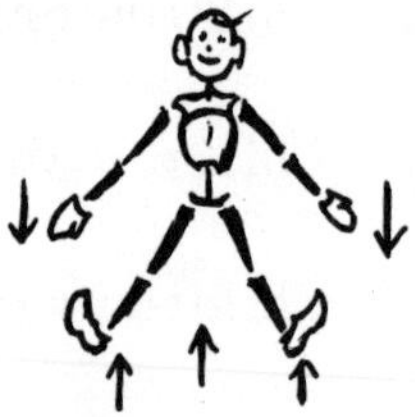

1. Children run with hands behind their back.
2. Children run on their tiptoes.
3. Children jump up and down with feet spread wide apart.
4. Children pretend to jump rope. Use both feet. Jump in place.
5. Each child jumps in place, using only one foot. Alternate feet.

1. Children, with feet together, jump forward one step.

2. Children, with feet together, jump backward one step.

3. Children jump forward three steps as teacher counts.

4. Children, with feet together, jump sideways (to left and to right).

1. Children jump and, while in air, turn. Turn one quarter of the way around.

2. Children jump and turn while in air. Turn one half of the way around.

3. With eyes closed, children jump and turn while in mid-air. Turn one quarter of the way around.

4. With eyes closed, children jump and turn while in air. Turn one half of the way around.

WEEK 11
FRIDAY

This day is to be used for an accumulative review of all basic body movement activities.

1. Children roll from their back to their stomach. They should be able to roll to the right and left on command.
2. Children walk sideways with arms folded on chest--use crossover step.
3. Children place heels together and walk.
4. Children place toes together and walk.
5. Children run with hands over head.
6. Children run with hands behind their backs.
7. Children jump forward three steps as teacher counts.
8. With eyes closed children jump and turn in the air--turn 1/4 and 1/2.

HEARING DISCRIMINATION

Many levels of ability in hearing discrimination exist in young children. Differences in this area may be due to native ability or early parental training.

Providing training for listening skills and discrimination between sounds can help many children overcome deficiencies in this area.

Unless training is given, many children will be unable to hear the teacher's instructions. Later problems in hearing and reading comprehension then may occur because the child has "tuned himself out."

Ask children to close eyes and listen as you clap your hands several times. Ask children to, "Clap just as I did." Vary this procedure by clapping in different rhythms. You may also use two drums, having children imitate the drum beats.

Suggested claps are:

three slow claps
two slow claps
two fast claps, pause, two fast claps
two fast claps, pause, one clap

Teacher stamps feet three times. Children, one at a time, imitate the rhythm and correct number of stamps.

Suggested variations of the rhythm:

two slow stamps
three slow stamps
two fast stamps, pause, two fast stamps
two fast stamps, pause, one stamp

Teacher claps hands twice and snaps fingers twice. Children, individually or in a group, imitate the actions. Begin with an even beat and progress to a syncopated rhythm.

Suggested rhythms:

one clap, one snap
three claps, three snaps
one clap, two snaps
two claps, one snap
one clap, three snaps
three claps, one snap

Using a tape recorder, encourage children to say their names, imitate animals, sing songs, etc.

Phonograph records may teach many sounds not easily accessible in the child's environment. Locate and use these records. Encourage children to discuss and name the various sounds.

This day is to be used for an evaluation of what the children have learned during the last week.

1. Teacher asks the children to close their eyes. They are asked to clap their hands in an imitation of the teacher clapping.

   a) clap three slow claps
   b) clap two fast - pause - two fast

2. Teacher stamps feet in varying rhythms - children, one at a time, imitate the rhythm.

   a) three slow stamps
   b) two fast stamps, pause, one stamp

3. Teacher claps hands and snaps fingers - children imitate.

   a) two claps - two snaps
   b) two claps - one snap
   c) one clap - two snaps

During quiet periods, the children should be encouraged to listen to the different sounds in the classroom. Examples: tick of the clock, a chair squeaking, coughs, shuffle of feet, etc. Discuss which sounds are louder, which are softer. Sounds from outside may be used in much the same way. Instead of doing this for an extended period of time do this several times throughout the day. In changing from one activity to another just say, "Stop, what do you hear?"

WEEK 13
TUESDAY

Select several rhythm instruments such as a drum, a triangle, a sand block, a wooden block, etc. Children watch as you make a sound on each. Ask the children to close their eyes and listen carefully. Strike a sound on one of the instruments. Have the children open their eyes and tell you which instrument you played. Next, have the children close their eyes and the teacher plays two instruments. Have the children tell you which instrument was played first, which one was played last. If the children comprehend this then play three instruments asking the children which were played first, second or last.

WEEK 13
WEDNESDAY

Give each child a toy animal. If you do not have enough toys, pictures may be substituted. Ask them to listen carefully. The teacher makes an animal sound. When they hear the sound their animal would make, they bring the toy or the picture to the teacher. Another way of doing this is to point to a child to make a sound. The one who has that animal must then switch animals with the one who called. It is then their turn to make a sound.

A good time for this activity is upon rising at nap time. While the children are still on their mats with the lights out the teacher deliberately makes sounds which the children identify. Some examples would be: jingling car keys, jingling money, moving a chair, tapping a pencil, closing a book, running fingers across the teeth of a comb, crumpling some paper, etc. Do not allow the children to see what you are doing. See if they know what you did.

Any of the activities from the previous week may be used. Choose an activity that the children had difficulty with or one they liked and understood.

Make sure you cover the following:

loud and soft
fast and slow
first and last
high and low

Using two wooden blocks or two rhythm sticks, place one on the table across the room. The teacher makes a series of taps by hitting one block or stick against a wooden surface. The children take turns, going across the room, picking up the block or stick and imitating the sound.

Example: tap three times, tap three quick times, pause, and two quick times, etc.

Place a number of objects on a table. Tap these objects in order to familiarize the children with the sound produced. Children should put their heads down. Tap an object and ask, "What is it?" After the children have become familiar with the objects tap several of them and ask them which you tapped first, which you tapped last.

WEEK 14
WEDNESDAY

Seat the children in a circle. Have one child leave the room. Give one of the children in the room a bell (one that is small enough to hide in his hand). Ask the child who left the room to come back in. When the child has returned have all the children stand and shake their fists above their heads. The child who returned must name the child with the bell. You may use more than one bell when the children become accustomed to the game.

Ask the children to imitate various human sounds. Examples: Laughing, singing, crying, shouting, whispering, etc.

Ask the children to imitate animal sounds. Examples: Barking, mewing, braying, crowing, cackling, etc.

Ask the children, "What are the sounds of weather?" Examples: wind, thunder, lightning, etc. Ask questions such as, "Does snow have a sound?" "What happens if we put two ice cubes in a glass and shake them around?"

This day is to be used for an accumulative review of hearing discrimination.

1. Children close eyes and imitate clapping sounds made by teacher.
   a) two fast claps, pause, two fast claps
   b) two fast claps, pause, one clap
2. Children imitate stamping sounds made by teacher.
   a) two fast stamps, pause, two fast stamps
   b) two fast stamps, pause, one stamp
3. Children imitate clapping and snapping sounds made by teacher, children keep eyes closed.
   a) one clap, three snaps
   b) two claps, one snap
4. Children close eyes and individually imitate a tapping sound made by the teacher using a block or rhythm stick.
   a) tap three times
   b) tap two times, pause, one time
   c) tap four times
   d) tap two times, pause, tap two times
5. Play the game described on Wednesday of Week 14.

SYMMETRICAL ACTIVITIES

For some children the difference between the right and left sides of the body has not been established. This can be due to too much emphasis being placed upon using the preferred side by parents.

Our bodies are structured so that we are designed symmetrically. It is felt that greater development of both sides of the body can lead to greater efficiency of movement and balancing ability.

WEEK 15
MONDAY

1. Children lie on their backs on the floor. Arms should be kept straight and at their sides. On command the children should slide their arms along the floor until they touch overhead. Remember that their arms should always be in contact with the floor.
2. Children lie on their backs on the floor. Arms should be straight and at their sides. On command the children should slide their arms along the floor until they can clap them overhead. Caution the children to keep their arms on the floor.
3. Children lie on their backs on the floor. Arms and legs should be straight. Arms at their sides and feet together. Slide arms up and legs apart simultaneously. Return to starting position. If this seems to be difficult for them try moving just the legs apart and back together again. After practicing this, try the arms and legs again.

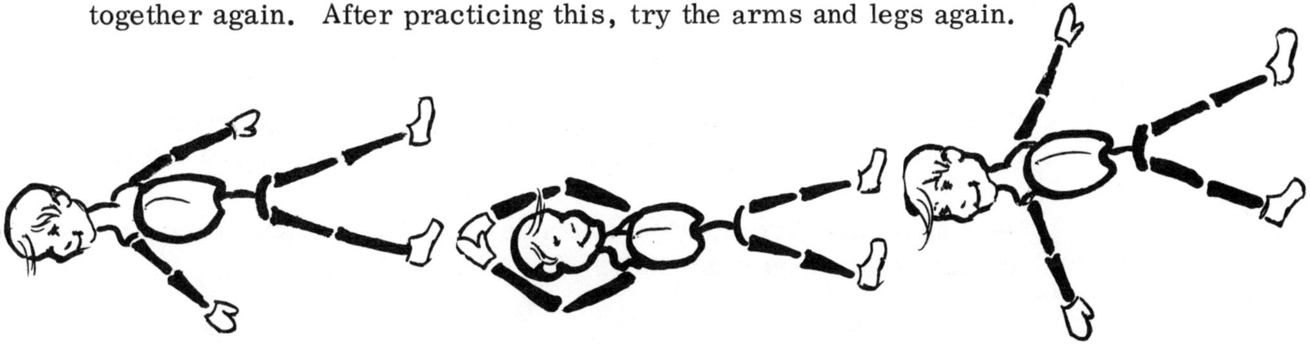

1. 2. 3.

1. Children lie on their back on the floor, arms straight and at their sides, feet together.

   Children slide right arm up, slowly and return. Repeat several times.
   Children slide left arm up, slowly and return. Repeat several times.
   Children slide right leg out, slowly and return. Repeat several times.
   Children slide left leg out, slowly and return. Repeat several times.

   Children should be able to do this without the other arm and leg moving. Only the prescribed member should move.

2. Children stand, feet together, arms at their sides.

   Children raise arms overhead until they touch. Repeat several times.
   Children raise arms overhead and clap hands. Repeat several times.

   Here again the children should be able to do this without overflow into the other limbs and to execute the moves smoothly.

1. Children lie on their back on the floor.
Children slide right arm up and right leg out, slowly. Return and repeat.
Children slide left arm up and left leg out, slowly. Return and repeat.
Only the members called for should be moved. There should be no overflow into other parts of the body.

2. Children stand.
Children use a jumping movement to move feet apart and together. Repeat several times.
Children use a jumping movement to move feet apart, at the same time, clapping hands overhead.
This activity should be done slowly and as proficiency increases the speed should be increased. Make sure that the feet are together when called for and not six inches apart.

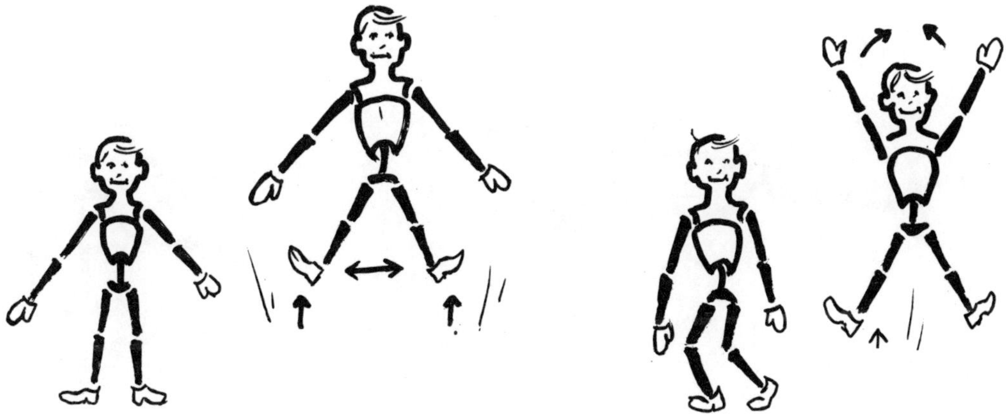

WEEK 15
THURSDAY

1. Children lie on their back on the floor, arms at sides and feet together.
Children slide right arm up and left leg out, slowly. Return and repeat.
Children slide left arm up and right leg out, slowly. Return and repeat.
Check the children again for overflow to other body members.

2. Children stand, arms at sides and feet together.
Children move right arm up and right leg out, slowly. Return and repeat.
Children move left arm up and left leg out, slowly. Return and repeat.
Children move right arm up and left leg out, slowly. Return and repeat.
Children move left arm up and right leg out, slowly. Return and repeat.
This activity should be done frequently so that there will be no hesitation in their movements.

1.

2.

WEEK 15
FRIDAY

This day is to be used for an evaluation of what the children have learned during the last week.

1. Children lie on their back on the floor. Slide arms and legs apart simultaneously.

2. Children lie on their back on the floor.
   a) children slide right arm up, slowly
   b) children slide left arm up, slowly

3. Children lie on their back on the floor
   a) children slide right arm up and left leg out, slowly
   b) children slide left arm up and right leg out, slowly

4. Children stand arms at sides and feet together
   a) children move right arm up and right leg out, slowly
   b) children move left arm up and left leg out, slowly

Children stand in a straight row. Teacher demonstrates while children imitate symmetrical arm and leg movements.

Children hop in a large circle. Be sure to use both feet.

Children stand in a straight row. Using hands and fingers, the children draw circles and lines in the air. Draw: in front, overhead, behind, and to the side.

Children lie on the floor. Children make circles in the air with arms. Children make circles in the air with feet.

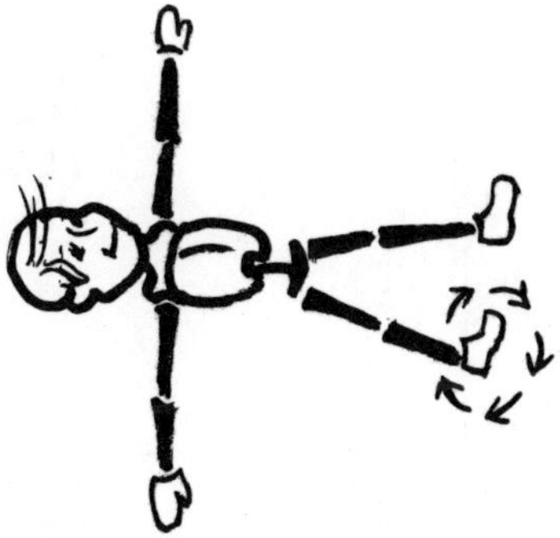

Imitate throwing - Children throw overhand, underhand, sideways, backhand (reach across the body), and both hands. Be sure all children use both hands alternately. A variation that includes strength and balance is to have children throw while standing on their knees.

Tug of War - Using a short rope, one child pulls against another.

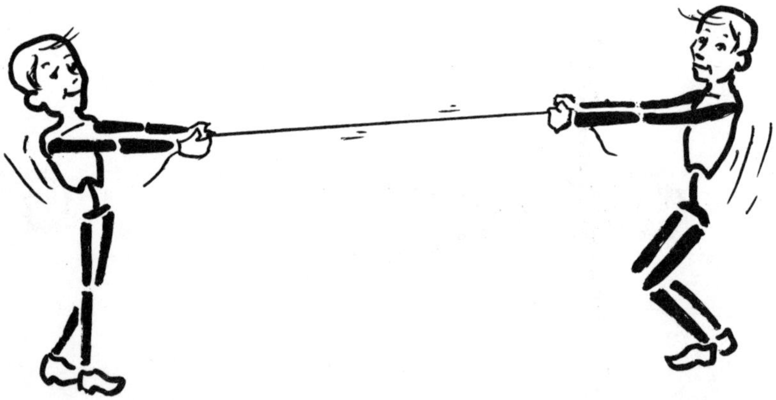

Imitate kicking - Children stand and kick on command. Alternate feet.
Pretend to kick a football. Alternate feet.
Kick backward. Alternate feet.
Kick sideways. Alternate feet.

Imitate swimming - Children pretend to swim by using the: crawl stroke, back stroke, breast stroke and side stroke.

This day is to be used for an evaluation of what the children have learned during the last week.

1. Children stand in a straight line. Teacher demonstrates while children imitate symmetrical arm and leg movements.
2. Children imitate throwing - overhand, underhand, backhand (reach across body). Be sure that both hands are used alternately.
3. Children imitate kicking - children stand and kick on command. Alternate feet.
   a) Kick forward
   b) Kick backward
   c) Kick sideways
4. Tug of War - Using a short rope, one child on each end, have the children pull against each other. Variation: Use a long rope, divide class in half and have them pull against each other.

WEEK 17
MONDAY

Have the children stand at the chalkboard with a piece of chalk in each hand. It is best to use the primary chalk if it is available. Hold the chalk at eye level. During this training, both hands should be used simultaneously. Have the child draw circular motions rotating counter-clockwise. Circles should be large. Ask the child to reverse and make circles going clockwise. The child's motions should be smooth and continuous. Next, have the child draw horizontal lines, going in and out from the center of the body. Here again the child's motions should be smooth and continuous.

As on Monday, the children are at the chalkboard. Remember the chalk should be held at eye level and the movements are to be made freely. Ask the children to draw lines going up and down. Have the hands move in the same direction. Both hands should start at the top and go down. An added dimension would be to do these activities in time to music.

Next, ask the children to draw vertical lines, this time alternating the arms. Start the left hand at the top and the right hand at the bottom. This is more difficult and should be tried but don't be upset if it isn't as smooth as the other.

If scooter boards are available have the children lie on their stomach and propel themselves forward using:

a) both arms simultaneously
b) both arms alternately

Have the child lie on his back and propel himself by:

a) pushing with both feet simultaneously
b) pushing with both feet alternately

If ropes are available have the children try to climb them. A swing set pole can be used as well.

Allow the children to ride tricycles.

Divide the class into two equal sides. Using a long clothesline rope (about 30 feet) have the children grab hold of the rope and pull tug-o-war fashion.

This time, tie the rope ends together and make a circle. Have the children stand in a circle around the rope. Have the children pickup the rope and on a given signal each child is to pull. Do not sustain the pulling for any longer than 10 seconds in either activity.

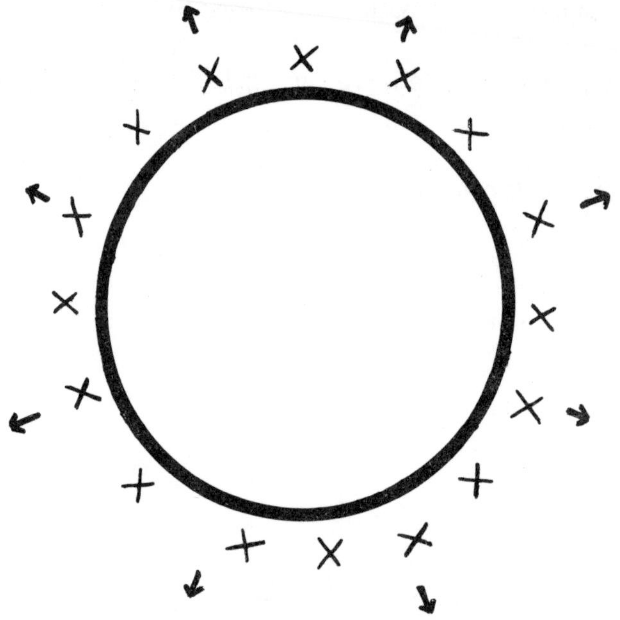

WEEK 17
FRIDAY

This day is to be used for an accumulative review of all symmetrical activities.

1. Children stand at chalkboard with chalk held at eye level, one in each hand. Have children draw circles with both hands.
2. Children imitate teacher kicking.
   a) Kick forward
   b) Kick backward
   c) Kick sideways
3. Children lie on their back on floor.
   a) children slide right arms up and left legs out, slowly
   b) children slide left arms up and right legs out slowly
4. Children stand, arms at sides and feet together
   a) children move right arms up and left legs out
   b) children move left arms up and right legs out
5. Tie the ends of a 30-foot clothesline together making a circle. Ask the class to stand holding the rope in front of them. At a given signal have children pull on the rope.

EYE HAND CO-ORDINATION

The combination of eyes and hands working together is necessary for achievement of many classroom experiences.

Many children lack the ability to visually steer their hands through space to accomplish an appointed task.

Training in this area will afford children opprotunities to practice the needed experiences necessary for the development of eye hand co-ordination.

WEEK 18
MONDAY

Place a large piece of newsprint or any kind of paper available in front of each child. Give each child a crayon. Ask the children to scribble. Encourage free movement and large movement.

After this experience you may put on a slow record and ask the children to scribble in time to the music. Turn the paper over and ask the children to scribble in time to a fast record. See if the children can distinguish the difference.

If time permits give the children a whole box of crayons and let them color the designs different colors. These make clever designs to hang on the bulletin board.

Using inflated balloons ask the children to keep them in the air by batting them with their open hands. See who can keep it up the longest.

Ask the children to stand in a circle. Let one child stand in the center of the circle. Have him bat the balloon in the air calling a name of a child in the circle. The child called must get into the circle and keep the balloon in the air while calling another name.

Have the children bat a balloon against the wall. See who can keep it going the longest.

Using a large playground ball or as many as you may have, ask each child to bounce the ball in front of himself and catch it with both hands.
When the child can do this quite readily, ask him to bounce the ball a certain number of times and stop. Make sure he does not exceed the number you requested.

Ask the children to bounce the balls continuously (dribble in one spot) using just the right hand.

Ask the children to bounce the balls continuously (dribble in one spot) using just the left hand.

Ask the children to bounce the balls continuously (dribble in one spot) alternating hands.

Ask the children to bounce the ball in front of them alternating hands left then right. See who can keep this up the longest. Have the child look at the ball while he is bouncing it.

Ask the children to throw the ball up in the air and catch it. See how many times they can do this in succession. Remember to have them keep their eye on the ball.
When the children can do this readily have them throw the ball up in the air and clap their hands one time before catching the ball.

Pair the children off and have them bounce the ball to each other. Make the distance between the children short at first, then back them up a little.

This day is to be used for an evaluation of what the children have learned during the last week.

1. Each child should have a balloon. Ask them to keep their balloons in the air by batting it with their hands.

2. Ask children to throw a playground ball in the air and catch it a number of times.

3. Ask the children to bounce the ball continuously using both hands.

Have the children stand in a circle with the teacher in the middle. The teacher should throw the ball underhand to each child in the circle. After going to each child in succession try to surprise the children by going randomly around the circle.

Hang a whiffle ball by a string from the lights or ceiling. With four children in a circle around each ball direct the children to keep the ball swinging by batting it with the palm of their hands.

Still using the whiffle ball in the same position designate one child to hit the ball and have the other children duck it. Let each child take turns at swinging the ball.

With the whiffle ball still hanging from the lights have the children take turns hitting the ball with a stick which is held with both hands.

Pegs and Pegboards

Each child should have a pegboard and some pegs. If you do not have enough to go around take small groups at a time while the others have free play or another scheduled activity.
Direct the children to place the pegs:

1. in the top row
2. in the bottom row
3. in the corners
4. on the right side
5. on the left side
6. in the middle

You may use this method to teach colors or numbers, too, while still training eye hand co-ordination.

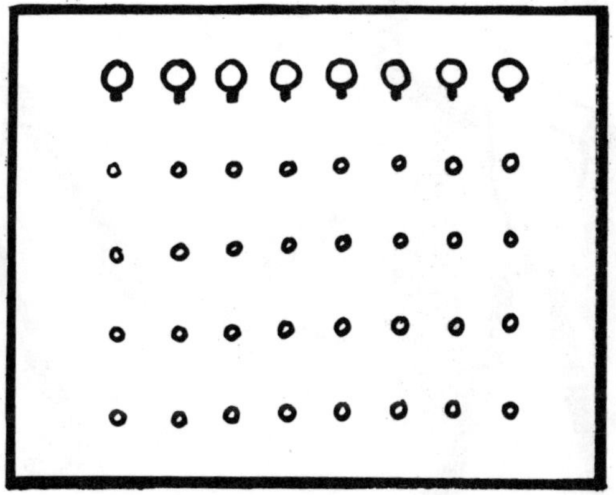

Bean Bags - Tossing bean bags can be done quite similar to ball activities. Bean bags can be tossed in the air to one's self, tossed from one hand to the other, tossed from one child to another, tossed underhand, overhand, etc.

A game may be contrived where the children toss bean bags into buckets or any container with a large opening. The container is placed 4-5 feet from the children. Numbers may be placed on the cans so they can learn to recognize and identify them. Older children might even be able to keep score if the numbers are not too large.

WEEK 19
THURSDAY

Place a series of small metal objects on the floor or on a table. Suspend some magnets from short pieces of string. While holding onto the end of the string have the children attempt to pick up objects by using just the magnets. At first let the children pick up any object they want. Later, specify an object to be picked up. At the beginning of this little game, place the objects far apart. As the children get used to the task, put the objects closer together to make it more difficult.

While one group is doing the above another group can be playing "Drop the Clothespin." From a standing position, children drop wooden clothespins into large mouth bottles. Make sure they hold the clothespin at waist height when dropping the pins.

This day is to be used for an evaluation of what the children have learned during the past week.

1. Children stand in a circle with the teacher in the middle. The teacher throws the ball to each child in the circle.
2. Pick up small objects with magnets on string.
3. Drop clothespins into large mouth bottles.
4. Toss bean bags in different ways as explained on Wednesday of Week 19.

WEEK 20
MONDAY

If you happen to have a workbench, one group of children can be hammering nails into pieces of wood, sawing or drilling holes into scraps of wood. When hammering do not use long nails. Use short nails with large flat heads. Hammers, saws and drills should be small enough for the child's hands.

While one group is at the work bench or area set up for such a purpose, another group can be at their tables stringing beads. The children may:

string beads randomly
string them by color
string them by shape
string them in a specific pattern
string them by number

WEEK 20
TUESDAY

Sewing Burlap - Using a dull pointed needle, yarn and some very course material such as burlap children sew. No pattern is necessary. Let the children sew randomly. Later on, when eye hand co-ordination is further developed, a specific pattern may be drawn onto the burlap for the children to follow. Needles may be made by cutting a clorox bottle into thin strips, pointing one end and making a hole in the other for the yarn.

Children play with "Barrel of Monkeys." (Commercial Game)

Ring Toss - Using rubber jar rings and coke bottles, or a commercial game, children throw the rings over the neck of the bottle which is placed four to five feet away. Here again numbers can be placed on the bottles and the older can be taught to recognize the numbers and to keep score.

The other children can work puzzles while waiting their turn on the ring toss.

Children should draw around geometric template (See Appendix) forms at the chalkboard. If proficient, they may repeat the same procedure on large paper with a crayon. Make sure the child stays in contact with the template at all times.

If you happen to have lacing boards or sewing boards the children may be divided up and those waiting for the chalkboard may be doing these.

Other commercial games you can use are "Chick-n-Egg," and "Billy and the Barrels."

WEEK 20
FRIDAY

This day is to be used for an accumulative review of all eye hand co-ordination activities.

1. Toss bean bags into buckets or any container with a large opening.
2. Pick up small objects with clothespins.
3. Draw around geometric templates at the chalkboard.
4. Sew Burlap - described on Thursday of Week 20.

EYE FOOT CO-ORDINATION

Control of movement through eye foot co-ordination is one of the most overlooked areas of development in young children. A child must be able to control the movement and direction of his body by using his legs and feet to the greatest advantage.

Our society in the past provided many opportunities for training in this area, but, day by day, these opportunities are rapidly decreasing.

We can make up for this deficiency by providing children with experiences designed to correlate visual steering with the movement of the feet.

WEEK 21
MONDAY

Place a strip of masking tape or length of clothesline on the floor. Direct the children to walk on the tape, making sure that feet touch the tape at all times.

Progression may be:

1. Children walk forward, heel to toe
2. Children walk forward on tiptoes
3. Children walk forward with giant steps
4. Children walk sideways each direction on tiptoes
5. Children walk backward

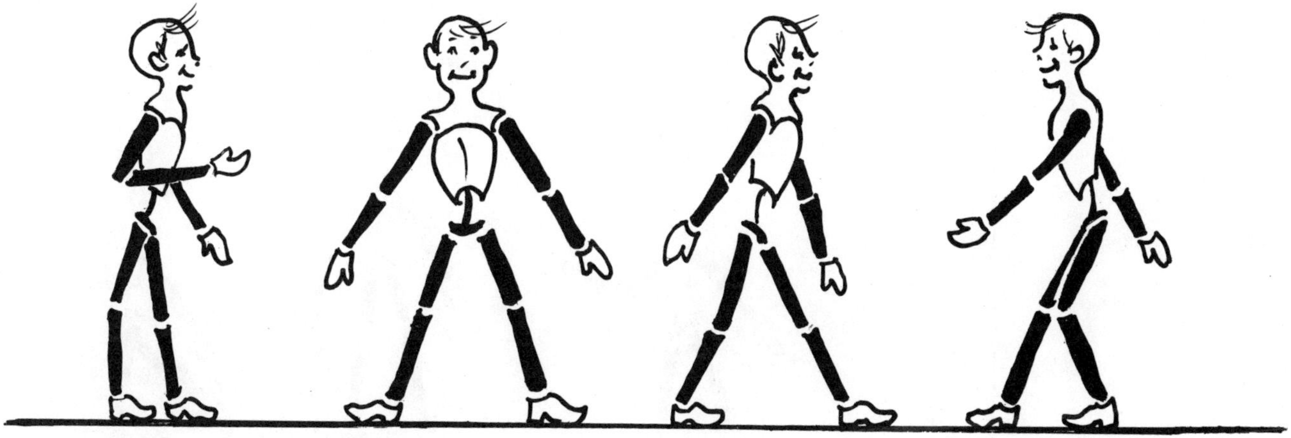

Place a strip of masking tape on the floor.

1. Children straddle the tape with feet as they walk.

2. Children use a crossover step, not stepping on the tape. Alternate left feet to right side tape and right feet to the left side of the tape.

Select objects of various heights, such as, boxes, blocks, small benches.
Place these so that the children can step over them without touching. You may want to start out with a single row of blocks on the floor and after everyone has stepped over add a layer each time. Note whether the children step over just enough to clear the blocks or whether they step an exaggerated height to clear the blocks. The first way is preferable. Later alternate objects that are high, medium and low, so they may judge the distance for themselves.

Lay pieces of clothes line in a loopy pattern on the floor and direct the children to step in the loops without touching the rope.

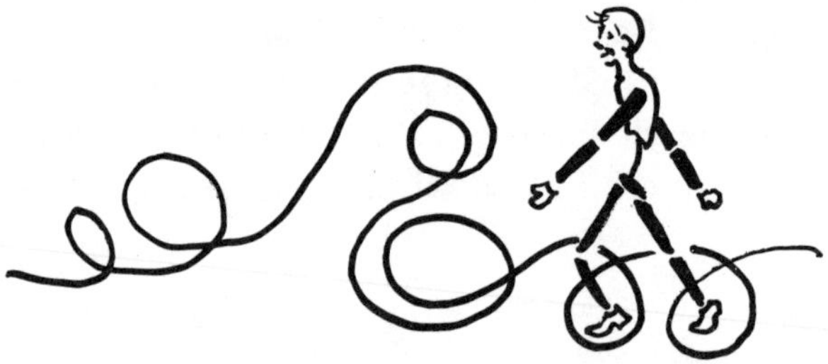

Optional: Trace footprints on a long piece of craft paper and ask children to step on each footprint. Vary the length of steps and the width of the steps. Crossover steps may be used.

WEEK 21
FRIDAY

This day is to be used for an evaluation of what the children have learned during the past week.

1. Use a strip of masking tape or length of clothesline on the floor.
   a) children walk forward - heel to toe
   b) children walk forward - tiptoes
   c) children walk sideways - tiptoes
   d) children use a crossover step

2. Select objects of various heights such as, boxes, blocks, etc. Ask children to step over them without touching.

WEEK 22
MONDAY

Children sit on chairs, facing a partner. Roll three inch balls back and forth between the partners. The ball is to be caught and rolled with the feet only. Use one or both feet. When children become more proficient at this task ask one child to move his chair back to make the distance between the children greater. This may also be done sitting on the floor. It might be wise to have the children take off their shoes for this activity enabling them to curl their toes around the ball when it is being caught.

Direct the children to push a bean bag across the floor with their feet. Children should learn to use both feet in doing this activity.

Progression for this activity may be:

1. Children push bean bag with right foot
2. Children push bean bag with left foot
3. Children push bean bag alternating feet
4. Run a race to a specific goal

Another approach may be to draw a circle or several circles in the middle of the floor and have the children stand on a goal at the end of the room. The children kick the bean bag toward a circle. Circles may be numbered and scores could be added up when someone gets the bean bag completely in the circle.

Snake - Wiggle a rope back and forth on the floor. Ask the children to jump over it without touching the rope "snake."

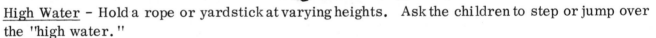

High Water - Hold a rope or yardstick at varying heights. Ask the children to step or jump over the "high water."

WEEK 22
THURSDAY

Children sit in a circle. Children attempt to keep an eight inch ball in the circle by kicking it with their feet. Do not let them touch the ball with their hands. Have the children lean back on their hands with their feet straight ahead. This cuts down on the possibility of the children using their hands and also frees their legs for more mobility.

This day is to be used for an evaluation of what the children have learned during the past week.

1. Have the children roll three inch balls back and forth to one another, catching and rolling them with their feet. Remember to take off their shoes.
2. Have the children push a bean bag with their right foot, left foot, and then, alternating feet.
3. Wiggle a long rope back and forth on the floor. Ask the children to jump over it without touching the rope "snake."

Jump the Shot - Swing a rope around your body in a circle of about eight feet. Children stand in a circle so that they may jump over the end of the rope when it comes to them. A weight is needed on the end of the rope to keep it on the floor. While doing this it is important, at least at first, to keep the rope moving at a constant pace. This makes it easier for the child and also helps to develop a sense of rhythm and timing. A bright colored object on the end of the rope will help the child identify the end he is to jump over. The key here is getting the child to keep his eye on the end of the rope and not on you. For those having extreme difficulty a verbal clue may be needed to get the child accustomed to the activity.

Children are instructed to hop from one spot on the floor to another, landing directly on the spot. Do not make the distance between the spots too great. These "spots" may be marked by chalk or tape squares. You may combine this motor activity with the teaching of colors, recognizing numbers or recognizing shapes. You may also line these spots up equi-distant from each other and have the child hop a certain number of times creating the necessity of counting objects. By allowing two children to jump using different numbers you could get across the concept of which number is more and which is less.

Stand children about six feet apart and have them kick an eight inch ball back and forth. The kicking motion should be soft and smooth. Be sure that the children kick with both feet alternately.

Optional: Children are taught to play hopscotch on the playground. Hopscotch boards may also be made with chalk or tape on the floor.

Ladder Walking - Children are instructed in the many different ways of walking on a ladder placed flat on the floor. Any flat ladder will do.

1. Walk forward with one foot on each side.
2. Walk forward on the right side of ladder. Return on the left.
3. Walk forward, stepping in the spaces between the rungs.
4. Walk backward, stepping in the spaces between the rungs.
5. Walk forward,stepping on each rung.
6. Walk backward, stepping on each rung.
7. Walk backward with one foot on each side.
8. Walk backward on the right side of the ladder. Return on the left.
9. Walk sideways, stepping in the spaces between the rungs. Use crossover step.

This day is to be used for an accumulative review of all eye foot co-ordination activities.

1. Place a strip of masking tape on the floor. Have the children:
   a) walk forward, sideways and backward.
   b) walk forward using crossover step
2. Children roll three inch balls back and forth to each other. Balls must be rolled and caught with their feet only.
3. Have children push bean bags with their feet:
   a) right foot
   b) left foot
   c) alternating feet
4. Play "high water" as described on Wednesday of Week 22.
5. Play "jump the shot" as described on Monday of Week 23.
6. Children walk on the rungs of a ladder and step in every other space of the ladder.

FORM PERCEPTION

Many children entering the first grade are presumed to have developed a recognition of various symbols and forms necessary to further academic achievement. Many studies show, however, that there are many children who need further training in this area.

Training can help children to develop a comprehension of basic forms; to perceive size, shape, straight and curved lines; and to be able to visually pick out an object against a background (figure-ground relationship).

WEEK 24
MONDAY

1. Use masking tape to make geometric shapes on the floor. Instruct children to walk around the tape outlines. Make circles, squares and triangles.

2. Create the various geometrical shapes by using the whole class. Children stand, or lie, forming the outlines of the figures.

1. Children trace around geometrical forms with fingers. Forms may be made of cardboard or small sticks glued on cardboard.

2. Children make shapes by using toothpicks or "pick-up sticks."

Place round, square and triangular objects into a bag or box. Children reach into the bag and tell which shape they are holding. Children remove the objects to see if they were correct. Try to secure things from as many rooms in the house as possible; kitchen, bathroom, playroom. Use as many objects as you can from the child's everyday world.

Cut large colored magazine pictures into geometrical shapes. Children must attempt to re-assemble them.

In order to make the created puzzle more durable and easier for the smaller children to fit together, mount the picture on construction paper or light weight cardboard. Then, cut your picture into the desired shapes. This also prevents curling up and tearing of the corners.

1. Use geometrical templates on chalkboard. Using chalk, children trace around the templates.

2. Cut geometric shapes out of construction paper. Place the paper shapes on a peg board. Children use pegs to outline the forms.

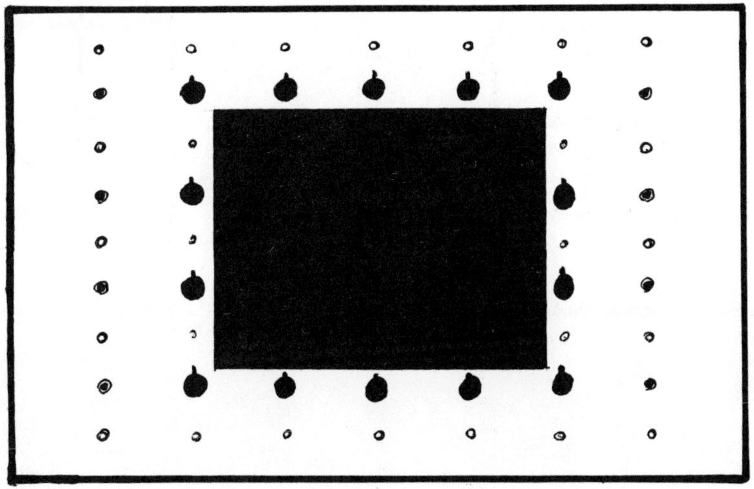

Children make geometric shapes out of building blocks. Let children copy yours and experiment. Use all dimensions. By this we mean that you can stack the blocks in various ways or make a shape with each block touching the table surface. When the child is copying your design make sure he sits so that he may readily see the shape from all angles. Those who are slower need to sit directly in front of you.

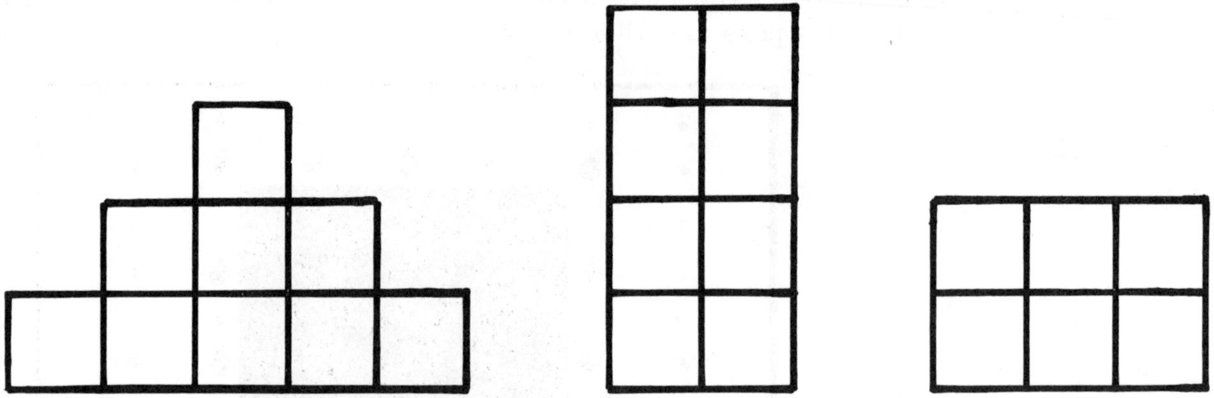

Create collage pictures using only geometrical forms. Use large forms which are easy for the children to cut out.

As an introduction to this session the teacher could put together several shapes making an object that would be familiar to the children - for example, a wagon.

Make reproductions of geometrical forms with missing lines. Have children try to complete the shapes.

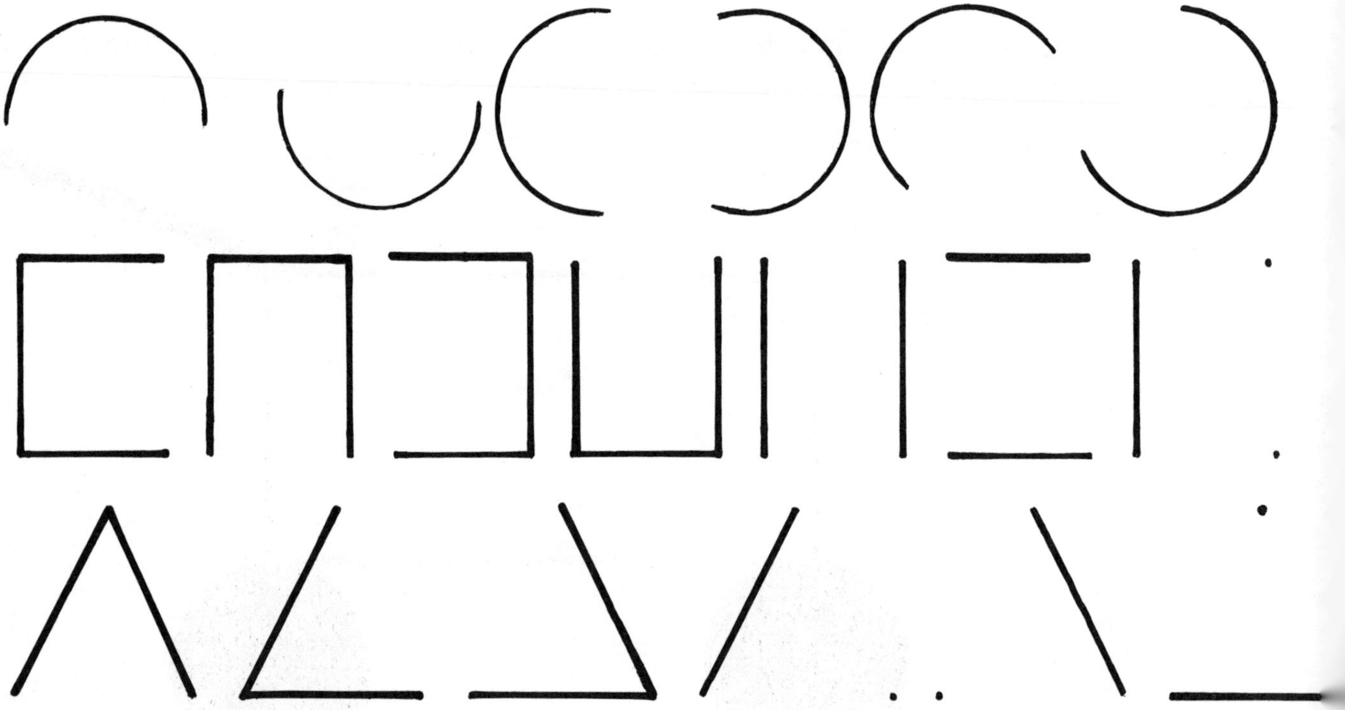

Play, "I See Something You Don't See."

Teacher starts by saying, "I see something _____________ (round, square, triangular, etc.). Can you guess what I see?"

Cut paper strips 1/2 inch wide. Give each child three or four strips of paper and ask them to paste strips on another piece of paper in the shape of a traingle or square.

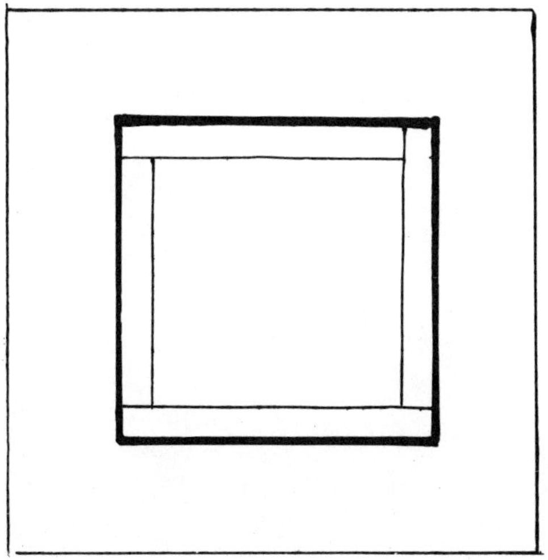

WEEK 25
FRIDAY

This day is to be used for an accumulative review of all form perception activities.

1. Place round, square and triangular objects into a bag. Have the children reach into the bag and tell which shape they are holding.

2. Children make shapes by using toothpicks or "pick-up sticks."

3. Make reproductions of geometrical forms with missing lines. Have children try to complete the shapes.

RHYTHM

Rhythm is the flow of bodily movement. It is through the development of rhythm, that the child can gain good muscle growth and motor co-ordination.

Basic locomotor rhythm (done to hand clap, drum beat, or music).

1. Children walk fast.
2. Children walk slowly.
3. Children walk with small quick steps.
4. Children walk with giant steps.

Basic locomotor rhythm (done to hand clap, drum beat, or music).

1. Children gallop.

2. Children run.

3. Children skate (gliding, slide step).

4. Children dance.

Basic locomotor rhythm (done to hand clap, drum beat, or music).

1. Children march.

2. Children jump in place.

3. Children hop across the room.

4. Each child hops on one foot across the room. Alternate feet.

5. Each child jumps, in place, on one foot. Alternate feet.

WEEK 26
THURSDAY

Body Rhythms: Children are asked to imitate repetitive rhythmic movements made by teacher or another child. Try to include every part of the body. Children make:

1. Clicking sounds with tongue.

2. Hands bend back and forth at wrist.

3. Elbows bend in and out from the body.

4. Shoulders shrug, while standing on knees.

5. One shoulder shrug, while standing on knees.

6. One leg raise and slap down on floor while lying on back.

7. One arm raise and slap down on floor while lying on back.

8. Just hands raise and slap down on floor while lying on back.

WEEK 26
FRIDAY

This day is to be used for an evaluation of what the children have learned during the past week.

First, use hand clapping and, then, follow with music. Have the children:

a) walk fast, then, slowly
b) gallop
c) run
d) skate
e) march
f) jump
g) hop

Children clap their hands together and slap their knees. Use the rhythms 1-1, 2-2, 3-3, and try 1-2, 2-1, 3-1, 1-3, 2-3, 3-2.

"Johnny Works with One Hammer" - Children sit on floor, legs stretched out in front.

(See Appendix for words and music.)

Children sit and listen to directions as given by teacher. Children follow these in a rhythm:

1. Clap hands twice and slap knees twice. Repeat.
2. Clap hands twice and touch head twice. Repeat.
3. Clap hands twice and touch elbows twice. Repeat.
4. Clap hands twice and slap stomach twice. Repeat.
5. Clap hands twice and touch ankles twice. Repeat.
6. Clap hands twice and pound chest twice. Repeat.
7. Clap hands twice and shrug shoulders twice. Repeat.

Teacher adds to these suggestions.

Using a table top, children beat out the rhythms: 1-1, 2-2, 3-3, 2-1, 1-2, 3-1, 1-3, 2-3, 3-2. Start this exercise by using each hand alternately. The teacher should beat these rhythms out and let the child imitate each.

On the last exercise, the children beat the rhythms with their hands. Repeat that exercise, using drum sticks.

Give each child a rhythm instrument. The teacher beats out the rhythms 1-1, 2-2, 3-3, 2-3, 3-2, 1-2, 2-1, 3-1, 1-3, on any rhythm instrument. The children who hold that particular instrument repeat the given rhythm. The teacher should be standing behind the children so that they are unable to see the instrument or the rhythm being beat.

WEEK 27
FRIDAY

This day is to be used for an evaluation of what the children have learned during the past week.

1. Ask the children to clap their hands together and slap their knees. Use the rhythms 1-1, 2-2, 3-3, 2-3, and 3-2.
2. Children sit and listen to directions as given by teacher. Use the following rhythms:
   a) Clap hands twice and slap stomach twice
   b) Clap hands twice and pound chest twice
   c) Clap hands twice and shrug shoulders twice
   d) Clap hands twice and touch elbows twice
3. Using a table top, children beat out the following hand rhythms. Children should start this exercise by beating out these rhythms with just one hand.
   1-1, 2-2, 3-3, 2-1, 1-2, 3-1, 1-3, 2-3, and 3-2.

LARGE MUSCLE ACTIVITIES

Large muscle activities start the child toward the development of his body for later life.

This training helps the child to have the ability to carry out daily tasks with vigor and alertness.

The emotional stresses placed on children in school situations can better be met if the child has a strong body.

Swaying - Children stand with arms overhead and lean to the left, right, front and back.

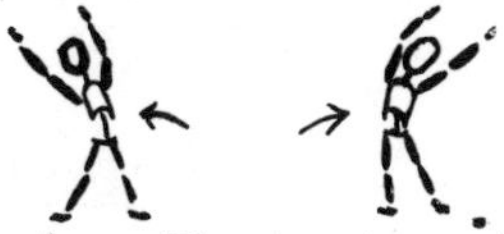

Parade Horses - Children walk forward, bringing knees very high in the air. Feet return to the floor, toes first.

Butterflies - Children extend arms and move them up and down in a graceful movement as they tiptoe around the room.

Frog Leaping - Children squat with hands on the floor in front of feet. They then leap forward, extending hands and bringing feet forward.

<u>Bend and Stretch</u> - Children stand with arms raised overhead. They then bend and touch their toes. Straighten and stretch up.

<u>Bunny Bounce</u> - Children hold hands straight up on both sides of their heads and hop forward by flexing knees.

Bend and Stretch

Bunny Bounce

<u>Swinging</u> - Children hold a partner's hand with arms slightly extended. Swing arms from side to side.

<u>Pony Ride</u> - Children squat, extend hands, pretending to be holding reins. Flexing knees, bounce up and down.

<u>Rag Doll</u> - Children bend forward, allowing arms to hang limp. Bounce upper body loosely. Legs remain stiff.

WEEK 28
WEDNESDAY

1. Knee Toe Touch - Children sit, legs spread wide apart. Bending forward from the hips, they touch their heads to their knees and fingers to the toes of one foot. Alternate to the other knee and foot.
2. Foot Head Touch - Children lie on the floor, keeping knees bent. Raise right foot to head and return to the floor. Repeat with the left.
3. Leg Stretch - Children lie on the floor, keeping knees bent. Raise both feet in the air. Straighten legs and return them to the floor, slowly.
4. Touching Toes - Children keep legs straight and bend forward from the waist to touch the toes.

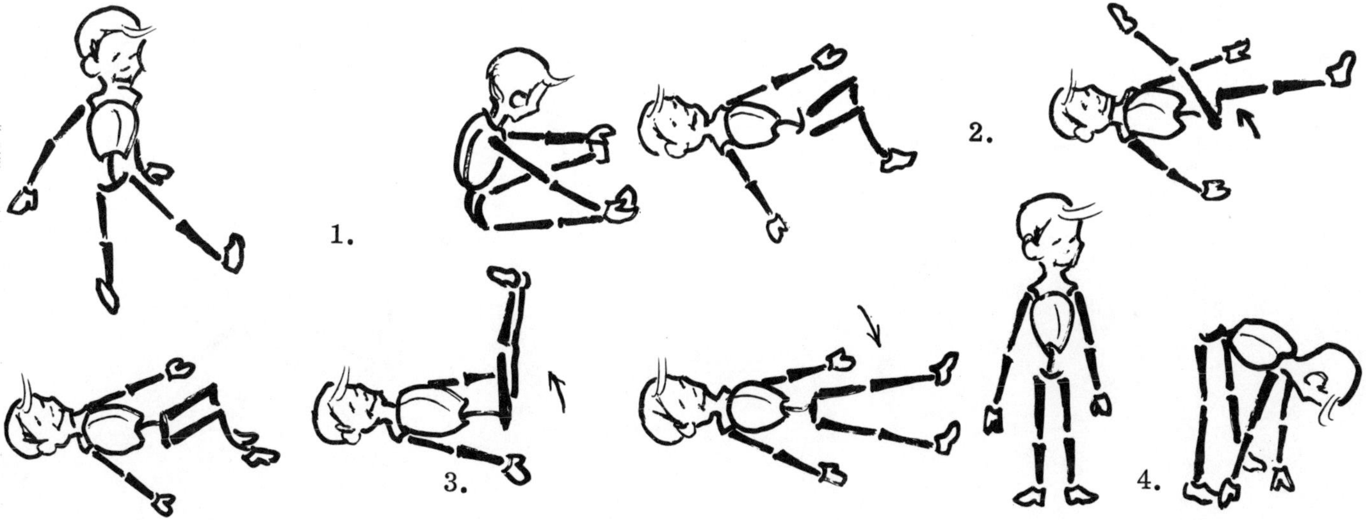

1. Torso Bends - Children place hands on hips and bend forward at the waist in a bouncing movement. Bounce to both sides.
2. Torso Twists - Children stand with arms stretched to the sides. Turn upper body as far to the right and left as possible.
3. Rowing - Children sit on floor, facing partner with soles of feet together. Children grasp each other's hands and alternately push and pull each other forward and backward.

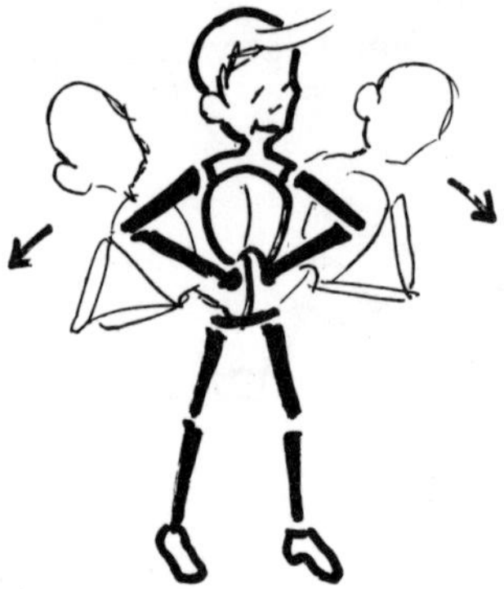

Seesaw - Children sit on floor, facing partner with soles of feet together. One child leans forward as the other leans back.

Sawing - Children stand and face their partner. Hold hands. Move hands alternately forward and backward.

Back Twins - Children stand back to back with elbows linked. From this position they attempt to sit down slowly and then try to stand again.

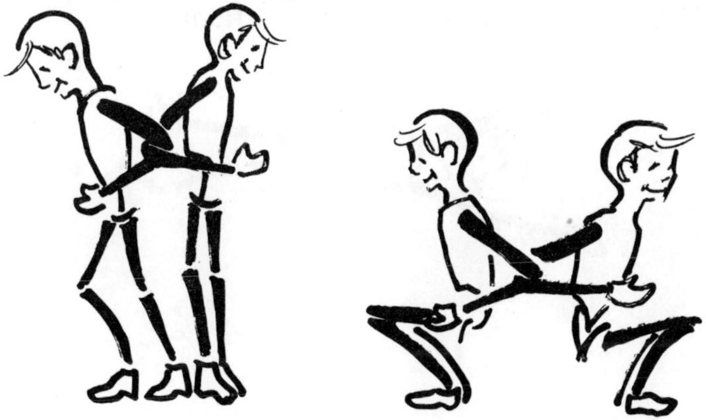

WEEK 29
MONDAY

1. Front somersault - Children assume a squatting position, roll forward and kick feet over head, finishing in a sitting position.

2. Back somersault - Children assume a squatting position, roll back and kick feet over head finishing in a kneeling position.

3. Bridge - Children lie on back and place hands on floor, over shoulders. Pushing with hands and feet, raise the body from the floor.

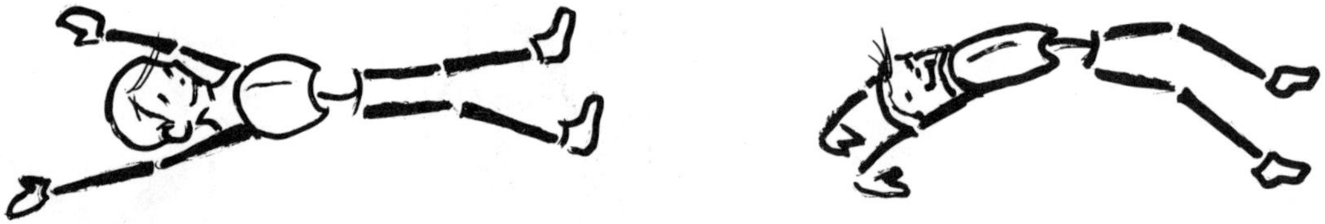

Wheelbarrow - One child lies on the floor on his stomach with legs spread. He places his palms flat on the floor near his shoulders. The second child stands between the legs and lifts the legs off the floor. The first child attempts to walk on his hands.

Yo-Yo Bounce - Children stretch arms straight out in front, bend knees and lower themselves to a squat position. They then straighten their legs and stand.

Leg Crossover - Children lie on their backs. Keeping the right leg in place, cross the left over the right and place the foot flat on the floor. Alternate legs.

Scissors - Children lie on their backs. Keeping legs straight, raise one leg and lower to floor. Repeat with the other leg.

Rolling Sit-Ups - Children lie on their backs. Feet are raised toward the head and then brought down forcefully, bringing the body to a sitting position.

Sit Ups - Children lie on their backs with arms stretched overhead. Arms are brought forward, raising the body from the floor.

Chest Stretch - Children open arms wide so that they are straight out of the shoulders. The arms are then brought forcefully forward, bending at the elbows, so that fists strike the chest.

Alternate Arm Action - Children stand with arms straight down at sides. Raise and lower right arm, then left arm. Keep arms straight at elbows.

Bicycle - Children lie on their backs with feet in the air. One leg is kept in the air, while the other is lowered toward the chest. Knees are bent when lowering. Alternate legs.

Shoulder Rotations - Children hold arms straight out to the sides. Turn palms up and then down. Repeat.

Arm Rotations - Children hold arms straight out at the sides. Keeping arms straight, move arms so as to make small circles with hands.

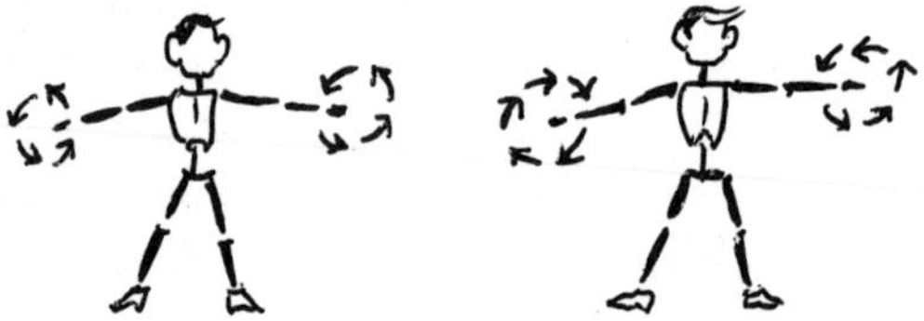

Ankle Rotation - Children lie with legs straight and toes pointed up. Turn feet so toes point in and then out.

Overhead Stretch - Children stand with arms at sides. Arms are then raised straight overhead. Children stretch toward ceiling. Lower arms and repeat.

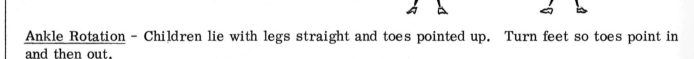

WEEK 30
MONDAY

Head Turn - Children lie on stomach, hands clasped behind back. Lift chest and shoulders off floor. Turn head to front, sides and as far to the back as possible without turning the body.

Flying Bird - Children lie on stomach and stretch arms like the wings of a bird. Lift and lower the head and chest while flapping the arms.

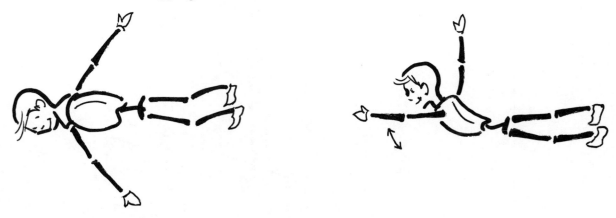

Floor Sweep - Children kneel and sit on their heels, hands on floor. Lean forward, sliding hands out in front until chest touches knees. In this position, swing arms to left and then to the right.

Slant Board Climbing - Children walk up and down a slanting board, without holding on. The slant on the board may be increased in subsequent turns for more difficulty. Variation: Children may creep up board on hands and knees or scoot up on the stomach.

<u>Ball Push</u> - Children assume a hand and knee position and push a ball along the floor with their heads.

<u>Siamese Twins</u> - Children face each other. Place foreheads together. Hold hands, with arms down straight. Walk backward, forward and sideways. Use various speeds in walking.

Knock 'Em - Facing a partner each child crosses arms on chest and stands on one foot. Hop to each other, trying to knock the other person off balance, using only the folded arms to push with. If both feet touch floor simultaneously, it is a knock down.

Hopping Kangaroo - Children assume squatting position and hop around the room imitating kangaroos.

Ball Passing - Children form a line, with arm's length distance between them. An eight inch ball is passed overhead from child to child. When the ball reaches the end of the line, the teacher takes the ball. The children are then asked to turn around and repeat the activity. Variation: Pass the ball through the legs or sideways.

Rope Jumping - Children can be taught to jump in the following ways:

1. Forward - feet together
2. Forward - alternate feet
3. Forward - one foot at a time
4. Backward - both feet together

Climbing Stairs - Children lie on their back with legs extended. Legs are made to imitate the climbing of stairs.

Rope Jumping -

1. Backward - feet together
2. Hot Pepper - forward jumping very fast
3. Hot Pepper - backward jumping very fast

Hand Leg Climb - Children lie on their back with one leg extended. Both hands are placed upon upper thighs and hands are then moved in a climbing manner toward ankles. As the hands move upward, the children sit up. Reverse and "climb" down the leg.

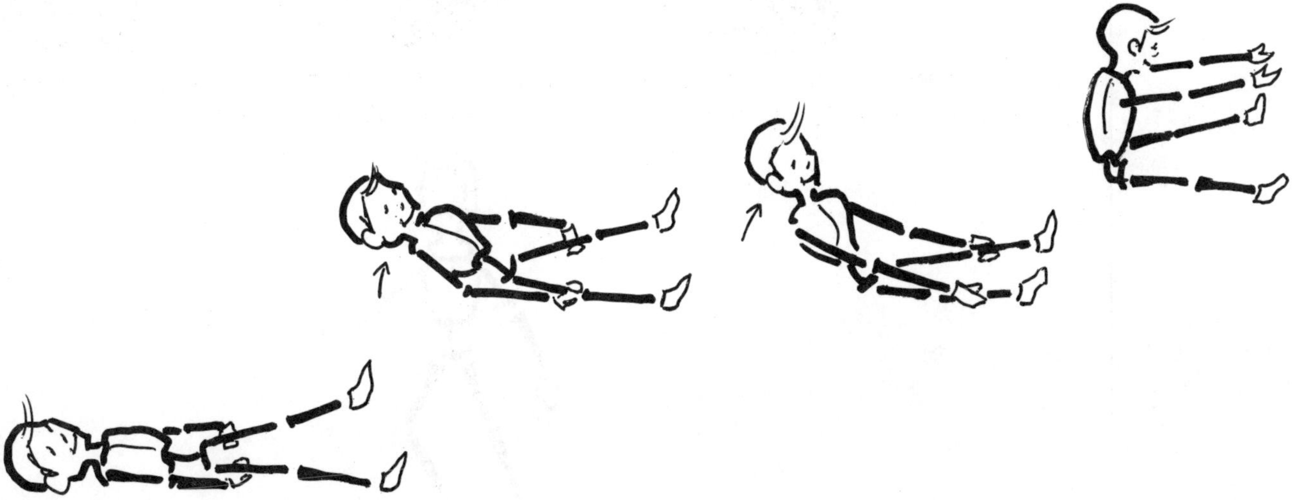

Backward Toe Touch - Children lie on their back, stretching their legs overhead until they touch the floor.

One Leg Swing - Children sit on the floor with one knee held to their chest. They then lie or roll backwards, bringing the other leg up into the air.

Ball Foot Roll - Place a three inch rubber ball under one foot. Roll the foot backward and forward over the ball, pressing down as hard as possible. Alternate feet.

Leg Push - Children sit facing a partner with soles of feet together. The children bend their knees and both push at the same time, trying to push each other away.

Toe Touch - Children lie on their back with a partner. The two heads touch at the top. Stretch arms overhead and hold hands. Legs are swung overhead until partner's toes are touched.

Stiff as a Board - Children assume a kneeling position with arms held stiffly at the sides. They then lean backward as far as possible, hold and straighten.

This day is to be used for an accumulative review of all large muscle activities.

1. Line the class up by twos making sure girls have girls as partners and boys have boys as partners. Have the first couple run to the teacher who is standing thirty yards away. The winner will go to the end of the line and the loser stands in back of the teacher. Each couple must run. Then pair off the winners as before and repeat the race until you have found the boy and girl winner.

2. After the racing have some jumping ropes, balls and climbing apparatus available so that the children may practice with this equipment on their own.

If the weather is nice it might be good to take the children outside for this review.

FINE MUSCLE DEVELOPMENT

During the pre-school years, a child develops hand muscle control in a rather aimless manner. Many parents and teachers fail to realize the necessity for training in this area. Therefore, many children are deficient in the areas of fine muscle and hand dexterity.

It is important to help children develop individual finger strength, finger coordination, and to begin their symmetrical training in the use of both hands.

In this section you will also find procedures for helping the children to gain controlled movement of the fine eye muscles. Many children need to develop more accuracy and control of their eye movements.

1. Children clasp hands so that the fingers of the right hand alternate with the fingers of the left. Change positions by placing the fingers of the right hand on the other side of the fingers of the left hand. Repeat several times.

2. Pick up small objects such as pennies, marbles, beans, straight pins, etc. Place these in the mouth of a small bottle or through a small opening in a box.

Children practice opening and closing a snap-type clothespin. When proficient at manipulating the clothespin, try picking up objects such as marbles, sticks, spring paper clips, pencils, small boxes, rubber bands, etc.

While seated, ask children to place their hands at arm's length about two feet apart with thumbs up. Holding head still, move eyes from left thumb to right thumb. Repeat several times.

Children imitate the movement of playing a pretend musical instrument. Form a band, march, and pretend to play.

While seated, ask the children to clasp hands so that both thumbs are up directly in front of the eyes. On command, without moving their heads, children move eyes from thumbs to a person or object in front of them. Reverse and repeat. Use as many objects in the room as possible. Proceed from larger to smaller objects.

WEEK 32
THURSDAY

Discuss several favorite stories with the children. Seat every child at the table and give each a piece of modeling clay. Instruct the children in making finger puppets of their favoriet character. Follow this activity by acting out the stories, using the finger puppets.

Fasten a light object such as a piece of chalk on the end of a string. Allow the object to swing slowly in front of each child's eyes. The child should attempt to track the piece of chalk with his eyes as it moves in front of him. Other children may watch to see if the eyes are moving correctly.

This day is to be used for an evaluation of what the children have learned during the past week.

1. While seated, ask children to place their hands at arm's length about two feet apart, with the thumbs up. Holding the head still, move eyes from left thumb to right thumb. Repeat several times. Move head very slowly.

2. Fasten a light object, such as a piece of chalk, on the end of a string. Allow the object to swing slowly in front of each child's eyes. The children should attempt to track the piece of chalk with their eyes.

3. Pick up small objects with fingers and drop into small bottle or box.

4. Use clothespins to drop objects into small bottles.

WEEK 33
MONDAY

1. Children close hands into tight fists. Open hands very wide. Repeat.
2. Holding hands up, palms facing teacher, children move thumbs in and out. Move fingers up and down. This should be done alternatingly.
3. Children hold hands vertically. Tap pointer fingers against thumbs. Tap five times. Tap middle fingers against thumbs five times, tap ring fingers against thumbs five times, and little fingers against thumbs five times. As the children readily sort out their fingers this exercise may be done to a drum beat, the ring of a triangle or to music. If the children have trouble in this area you may need to do this one hand at a time.

1. Children clap fingertips together.

2. Children snap fingers. Until proficient, each child uses only one hand at a time.

3. Have children place a pencil in their right hand. With the pointer finger and thumb of the left hand pick up the pencil slowly raising it to eye level, then lowering it back to the right hand and releasing it. Eyes should follow the pencil up and down. Pick up the pencil again, this time with the middle finger and thumb and repeat the process of raising and lowering the pencil. Next, pick the pencil up with the ring finger and thumb and then with the little finger and thumb. After each finger on the left hand is used place the pencil in the left hand and repeat the whole cycle using the right hand.

1. Place a half sheet of newspaper in front of each child. Children should be sitting at their desks, with one hand behind their chair. With the free hand the children should pick up the paper and start to crumple it into a small ball. They may not touch their bodies to aid them in crumpling the paper nor may they touch the desk. The hand should be held directly in front of them. When the paper disappears into their hands allow the children to smooth out the paper with both hands and repeat the task with the other hand. You may continue the task as long as the paper and the children's interest will allow.

2. Children place fingertips of right hands against those of the left. Keep fingertips together and clap palms. Release and repeat.

3. Children place palms of right hand on table. Each child taps his pointer finger on the table without moving the other fingers. Tap five times. Tap the middle finger on the table five times without moving the other fingers. Repeat with the ring finger then the little finger. Upon completion of the cycle repeat with the other hand. When children are able to do this well, they may do both hands at the same time.

1. Children cross middle fingers over pointer fingers. Reverse with pointer fingers over middle fingers. Use both hands. Cross index fingers over thumbs. Reverse with thumbs over index fingers.

2. Children grasp hands with fingers of right hands between thumbs and pointer fingers of left. Change so that left fingers are between right thumbs and pointer fingers. Repeat.

3. Each child tosses a bean bag from one hand to the other while holding head still and watching the bean bag.

WEEK 33
FRIDAY

This day is to be used for an evaluation of what the children learned during the past week.

1. Repeat exercise Number 3 on Page 161.

2. Ask children to place fingertips of right hands against those of the left. Keep fingertips together and clap palms.

3. Repeat exercise Number 3 on Page 163.

4. Repeat paper crumpling activity. If possible this activity canbe repeated daily to develop strength in the hand muscles.

Children sit in chairs and remove shoes and socks. Place their socks in front of them. Without moving heels from the floor, extend the toes so as to grasp the stocking. Pull a piece of it under the foot. Repeat until the stocking is completely under the foot. Alternate feet.

Hold balloons above children's heads and release. Children catch them. Be sure that they watch the balloon as it falls.

Children sit in a circle on the floor. Give one child a ping-pong ball. Move the ball about the circle by:

1. Flipping the ball, using thumbs and pointer fingers.
2. Batting the ball with the back of the hands.
3. Batting the ball with the front of the hands.

Children sit in chairs and put point of toes on floor. "Pretend you are a ballerina dancing on her toes." Move toes about as if taking tiny steps.

Place a selection of small objects on the floor. Examples: jacks, marbles, small balls, crayons, pencils, pegs, etc. Children use their toes to pick up the objects and place in a box.

Children sit in chairs and stretch right leg out in front. Place sole of left foot against the cal of right leg. Massage, using toes and heels. Alternate feet.

Children sit on the floor with legs outstretched in front. Keeping heels on the floor:

1. Children bend toes up and down.
2. Children spread toes apart and together.
3. Children try to cross their toes.
4. Children place their big toes on the floor. Wiggle other toes.

Teacher crumples a piece of paper and places it in the center of the table. Children kneeling around the table attempt to blow the paper. Variation: Children form circles and lie on their stomach. Attempt to blow the crumpled paper out of the circles.

This day is to be used for an accumulative review of all fine muscle development activities.

1. Fasten a light object, such as a piece of chalk, on the end of a string. Allow the object t swing slowly in front of each child's eyes. The children should attempt to track the piec of chalk with their eyes.

2. Repeat exercise Number 3 on Page 161.

3. Repeat exercise Number 3 on Page 163.

4. Place a selection of small objects on the floor. Children use their toes to pick up the ob jects and place in a box.

5. Teacher crumples a piece of paper and places it in the center of the table. Children kneel ing around the table attempt to blow the paper.

GAMES

1. Brownies and Fairies - The players are in two groups: one called Brownies, the other Fairies. Goal lines are marked across both ends of playing area. Each group, in turn, stands on its goal line with the players' backs turned toward the other group. Upon a silent signal from the teacher, the Brownies (or Fairies) advance quietly toward the other group's goal line. When they are within approximately ten to fifteen feet, the teacher calls, "The Brownies (or Fairies) are coming." This is the signal for the Fairies to turn and chase, until the group is safe behind their goal line. Those who were tagged before reaching the goal line, go with the children of the other team and become members of that team. Repeat with the other team.

   Develops: Directionality, space relationships, hearing discrimination.

2. Call Ball - The players stand in a circle with one child in the center. The child in the center tosses the ball above his head while calling the name of a child in the circle. The child whose name was called tries to catch the ball. (It may be necessary to let the ball bounce several times until the children get used to the game.) This child then takes the place of the child in the center.

   Develops: Eye hand co-ordination, hearing discrimination, large muscle co-ordination.

3. Back-to-Back - The players are arranged in couples. Partners stand back-to-back with elbows linked. One extra player does not have a partner. Upon a signal from the teacher, all players change partners while the extra player attempts to get a partner. One player will be left each time. The game is repeated with the player who is left without a partner giving the signal for the next change.

   Develops: Body image, directionality, spatial relations.

4. <u>Charlie Over the Water</u> - The players are in a circle with hands joined. One player, "Charlie," stands in the center of the circle. The players walk around in a circle chanting:

Charlie over the water,
Charlie over the sea,
Charlie caught a blackbird
But he can't catch me.

As they say "me" the players squat quickly. "Charlie" tries to tag a player before he squats down. If he is successful, the child whom he tagged changes places with him and the game is repeated with a new "Charlie."

<u>Develops</u>: Large muscle co-ordination, directionality.

5. <u>Dog and Bone</u> - One child is selected to be the dog. He sits on a chair in front of the children who are sitting at their desks. The dog closes his eyes. His back is toward the other players. The dog's bone, which is an eraser or any small article, is placed near his chair. A child selected by the teacher attempts to sneak up to the dog and touch his bone without the dog hearing him. If the dog hears someone coming, he turns toward the person and says, "Bow-Wow." Then, the player must return to his own seat and another child tries. If this child is successful in touching the bone before the dog hears him he becomes the dog and the game is repeated.

<u>Develops</u>: Hearing discrimination, fine muscle development.

6. <u>Crossing the Brook</u> - Two lines are drawn to represent the banks of the brook. The children run and jump over the brook. Anyone missing the jump and landing in the brook is sent "home" to put on dry shoes and socks; he sits and pretends to do these things, then re-enters the game.

<u>Develops</u>: Hearing discrimination, directionality, spatial relationship, balance, eye foot co-ordination.

7. Who Has Gone from the Room - The players sit in their seats or in a circle. One child is "IT." He closes his eyes while the teacher indicates which child shall leave the room. After this child has gone, the child who is "IT" opens his eyes and guesses who has gone. If he fails to name the child, he closes his eyes again, the child returns to the room, and "IT" opens his eyes and guesses who has returned. If he fails, he must be "IT" again.

Develops: Visual memory.

8. Huckleberry Beanstalk - Some small object is hidden by the teacher while the players are outside of the room. They are called in to hunt for the hidden object. Anyone seeing it takes his seat and calls, "Huckleberry beanstalk." The object of the game is not to be the last to find the object.

Develops: Eye movement.

9. I'm Going to Catch a Fish - Place children seated in a circle, one child in the middle, "the fish." Child in the circle holding a large ball says, "I'm going to catch a fish!" Child in the middle says, "Oh no you're not!" Child in circle rolls or throws the ball and tries to hit the fish. When the fish is hit, he sits in circle. The child who has hit the fish becomes "the fish."

Develops: Directionality, eye hand co-ordination, large muscle development.

10. Duck, Duck, Goose - Place children in circle. One child walks around outside of circle touching each child on head, saying "Duck." When he comes to a person he wants to chase him, he taps him and says, "Goose." The person tapped chases the "Duck" around the circle. The "Duck" must get back to the person's place before he is tabbed. If tabbed, he must go into the middle of circle.

Develops: Large muscle development, directionality.

11. Circle Stride Ball - Use large ball (volleyball). Players stand in circle with feet touching on both sides. One child is "IT" and stands in center. He tries to roll ball through the feet of any child in the circle. If he succeeds, he takes the place of the child and this child becomes "IT." Children can use only hands to stop the ball.

Develops: Basic body movement, eye hand co-ordination.

12. Teacher Ball - Use 6 to 8 players. One child is "Teacher" and players line up about 5 feet from "Teacher" in a straight line. "Teacher" throws ball, underhand, to each child in turn. If a player misses, he goes to end of line and child at head of line becomes "Teacher."

Develops: Eye hand co-ordination, direction.

13. Squirrel and Nut - Children place heads on desk, right hand open on desk. One child is squirrel and drops the nut (a piece of chalk) into the hand of a child. The child immediately gets up and tries to tag squirrel, who is safe if he can get back to the seat vacated by the second child.

Develops: Hearing discrimination, fine muscle development.

14. Seven Jumps - Circle to the left seven steps - stop. Circle to the right seven steps - stop. Raise right foot - hold. Put it down. Circle to left seven steps then back to right seven steps - stop. Raise right foot, put it down. Raise left foot, put it down. Circle to left seven steps then back to right seven steps - stop. Raise right foot - hold, put it down. Raise left foot, hold, put it down. Kneel on right knee. Stand. Circle to left seven steps then back to right seven steps - stop. Raise right foot - hold. Put it down. Raise left foot - hold. Put it down. Kneel on right knee. Kneel on left knee. Stand. Circle to left seven steps then back to right seven steps - stop. Raise right foot - hold. Put it down. Raise left foot - hold. Put it down. Kneel on right knee. Kneel on left knee. Put one elbow on floor. Stand. Circle to left seven steps - stop. Circle to right seven steps - stop. Raise right foot - hold. Put it down. Raise left foot - hold. Put it down. Kneel on right knee, kneel on left knee. Put one elbow on floor, put other elbow on floor. Stand. Circle to left seven steps then back to right seven steps - stop. Raise right foot - hold. Put it down. Raise left foot - hold. Put it down. Kneel on left knee. Kneel on right knee. Put one elbow on floor, put other elbow on floor. Touch head to floor. Stand. Circle to left seven steps then back to right seven steps - stop.

15. Looby Lou	Develops:	Body Image
16. Jack Be Nimble	Develops:	Eye foot co-ordination
17. Did you Ever See a Lassie?	Develops:	Body Image
18. Hokey Pokey	Develops:	Body Image, Direction, Hearing Discrimination
19. Bow Bow Belinda	Develops:	Symmetrical activities, Large muscle development, Body Image
20. Put Your Finger in the Air	Develops:	Body Image
21. Rainy Day	Develops:	Basic Movement
22. Join in the Game	Develops:	Hearing Discrimination, Basic Movement

APPENDIX

"Johnny Works With One Hammer" (Folk Song)

1. Johnny works with one hammer, one hammer, one hammer
   Johnny works with one hammer, then he works with two.
2. Johnny works with two hammers, two hammers,two hammers
   Johnny works with two hammers, then he works with three.
3. Johnny works with three hammers, three hammers, three hammers
   Johnny works with three hammers, then he works with four.
4. Johnny works with four hammers, four hammers, four hammers
   Johnny works with four hammers, then he works with five.
5. Johnny works with five hammers, five hammers, five hammers
   Johnny works with five hammers, then he goes to sleep.

Verse one:	Pound hand on floor.
Verse two:	Pound two hands on floor.
Verse three:	Pound two hands and one foot on floor.
Verse four:	Pound two hands and two feet on floor.
Verse five:	Pound two hands and two feet on floor and nod head.

DEVELOPMENTAL EQUIPMENT

Required

- Paper and Crayons
- Chalkboard
- Walking Board
- Balance Board
- Ladder
- Twist Board
- Clothespins
- Small Bells
- Masking Tape
- Rope
- Geometric Templates
- Bean Bags
- Playground Ball (8 inch)
- Ping Pong Ball
- Rubber Ball (3 inch)
- Mats
- Blocks
- Whiffle Ball
- Balloons
- Magnets
- Peg Board

- -

Optional

- Puzzles
- Work Bench
- Ring Toss Game
- Clay
- Beads
- Burlap and Needles
- Sewing and Lacing Boards
- "Chick-n-Egg" Game
- "Billy and the Barrels" Game
- Finger Paints
- Drums
- Rhythm Band Instruments
- Tape Recorder

Suggested ACTIVITY and HONOR YOUR PARTNER records to use in conjunction with this manual.

Rhythms for Today	Album 29
Finger Games	Album 506
Rope Skipping	Album 12
Modern Dynamic Physical Fitness Activities	Album 14
Basic Rhythms	Album 102
The Development of Body Awareness and Position in Space	Album 605
Basic Concepts through Dance	Album 601

BALANCE BOARD

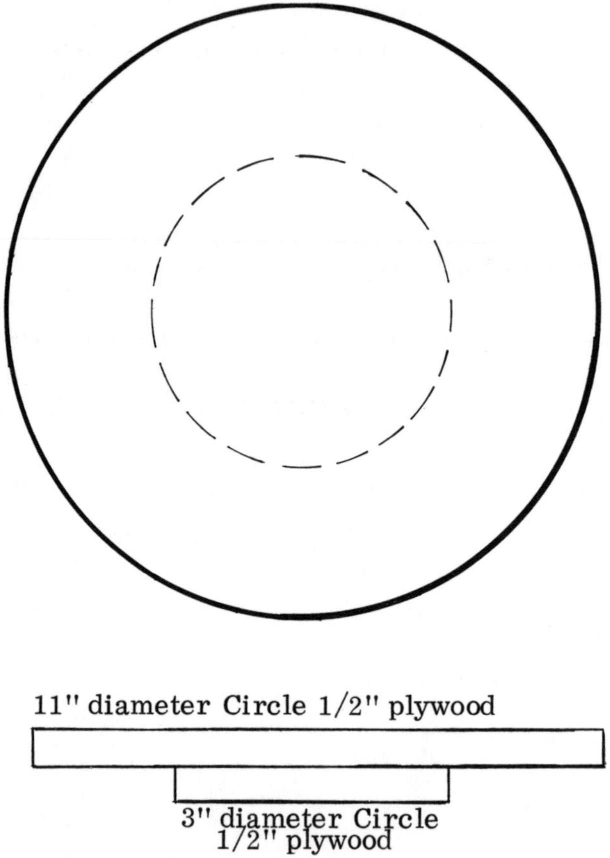

GEOMETRIC TEMPLATES

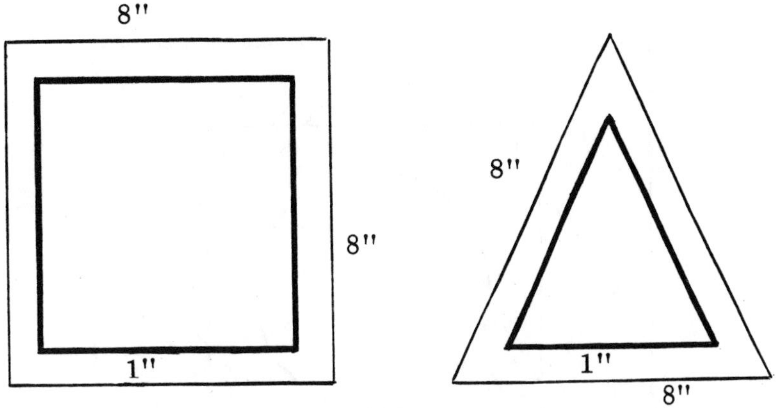

Cut out of heavy cardboard or Masonite

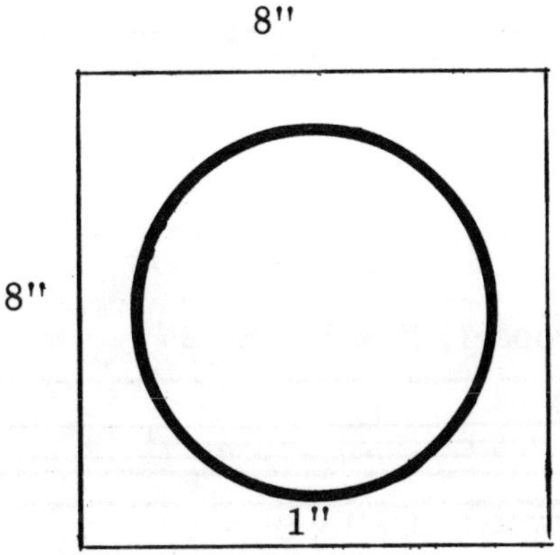

TWIST BOARD

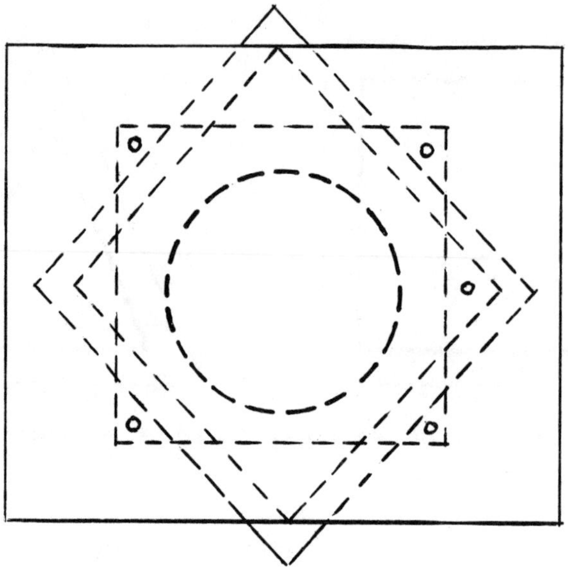

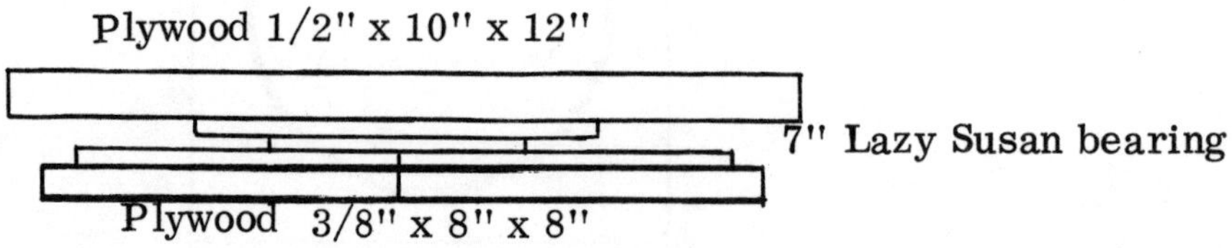
Plywood 1/2" x 10" x 12"
7" Lazy Susan bearing
Plywood 3/8" x 8" x 8"

WALKING BOARD

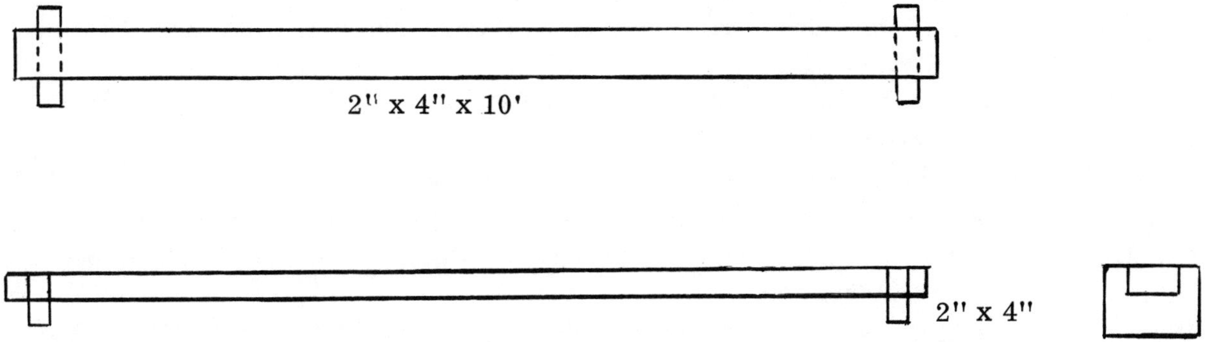

BIBLIOGRAPHY

Barsch, R.H., Ph.D. A Movigenic Curriculum. Madison, Wisconsin, 1965. Bulletin No. 25. pp. 57.

Board of Education of the City of New York. Physical Activities for Elementary Schools. New York, New York, Board of Education, 1958.

Brodrick, M., Counts, C., Dunbar, M. Self-Testing Unit - Primary Level. Santa Rosa, California, Sonoma County Schools. pp. 13.

Clements, S.D., Ph.D. Minimal Brain Dysfunction in Children. U. S. Department of Health, Education and Welfare, 1966. Monograph No. 3. pp. 18.

Cratty, B. J., Ed.D. Developmental Sequences of Perceptual Motor Tasks. Freeport, New York, Educational Activities, Inc., 1967.

Department of Elementary-Kindergarten-Nursery Education, National Education Association of the U.S. Prevention of Failure, 1965. pp. 92.

Demeter, Rosa. Hop-Run-Jump. New York, New York, The John Day Company, 1968.

Detroit Public Schools-Board of Education. First Steps in Language Experiences for Pre-school Children. The Duplicating Section, Department of Publications, Division of School Relations and Special Services, 1966. pp. 95.

Getman, G. N. How to Develop your Child's Intelligence. Luverne, Minnesota. G. N. Getman, 1962.

Getman, G. N., Kane, E. R. The Physiology of Readiness. P. A. S. S., Inc., 1964. Contributing authors: Halgren, M.R., McKee, G. W.

Kephart, N.C. The Slow Learner in the Classroom. Columbus, Ohio, Charles E. Merrill, Inc., 1960.

Lambeth, J., M.Ed. What Optometry and Its Related Fields Have to Offer the Reading Teacher. Optometric Extension Program, Duncan, Oklahoma, Research Paper 1966. pp. 61.

Bibliography (continued)

LeCrone, H., LeCrone, M.J. Physical Fitness for Pre-School Children. Oklahoma City, Oklahoma, Rhythm Record Company. RRC - 703.

Optometric Extension Program. The Primary Visual Abilities Essential to Academic Achievement. Duncan, Oklhaoma, Optometric Extension Program, 1964. pp. 42.

Prudden, Bonnie. How to Keep Your Child Fit from Birth to Six. New York, Evanston, London, Harper and Row, 1964.

Randler, D. H. and Kephart, N.C. Success Through Play. New York, N.Y., Harper and Row, 1960.

OTHER RECORDS IN PERCEPTUAL I
Available from E

Learning Basic Skills Through Music

Individualization in Movement and Musi

Modern Tunes for Rhythms and Instrum

Creative Movement and Rhythmic Explo

Sensorimotor Training in the Classroon

Perceptual-Motor Rhythm Games

To Move Is To Be

Music For Movement Exploration

Developing Perceptual-Motor Needs of I